THE LUCK WE CARRY

LOVE, LOSS, AND THE STORIES THAT SHAPE US

RON STEMPKOWSKI

For Ken. Always.

*And for the new versions of ourselves
we sculpt from the ashes of love and grief,
bruised but undaunted.*

CONTENTS

I met Ron Stempkowski during one of the most difficult seasons of his life. I could tell right away that he was utterly exhausted, deeply sad, and grappling with the kind of anxiety and fear that so often haunt caregivers. And yet even then, he glowed with a gentle, luminous quality that I found comforting.

Having been a caregiver myself, I felt I understood his experience in an intimate way. But when I met his husband, Ken, the person Ron was caring for, my heart immediately broke for both of them. Even though I was meeting Ken at the very end of his life, and Ron during one of the hardest moments of his, it was abundantly clear what a beautiful and loving couple they were, and that together they had created a magical life.

It became a strange privilege, as it so often does in my line of work, to encounter these two souls at the close of their relationship. I was just thirty-two years old when I first walked into Ron and Ken's apartment. At the time, I was a young wife, a new mother, and the bereavement counselor for a small hospice on the north side of Chicago.

Looking back almost two decades later, I can hardly believe

how young I was when I began that work. I had taken the position thinking I knew quite a lot about grief, but I realized very quickly that I only knew *my* grief, *my* experiences of death and loss. In those early years working in that snowy Chicago hospice, I learned something new every single day. But it wasn't that I was learning so much about death as I was learning about life and love and relationships.

My days were spent driving all over Chicago's north side and surrounding suburbs, visiting patients in their homes, hospitals, and skilled care facilities. Sometimes a patient was alone in a medical room, lonely and nearing death without family nearby. Other times, I entered homes filled with loved ones and caregivers gathered around a hospital bed in the living room. I never quite knew what I would encounter, and I learned to arrive open to whatever was waiting for me.

I sat beside dying people holding their hands without knowing anything about the lives they had lived. I listened to some of the last thoughts they would ever share in the world — regrets, fears, wishes that never came true, gratitude for the places they traveled and the people they loved. Just as often, I found myself sitting at kitchen tables with caregivers, drinking mugs of stale coffee while an exhausted spouse sobbed in my arms, overwhelmed by the weight of caregiving and the looming grief ahead.

To me, it was sacred work.

Not only because I had once been on the receiving end of someone like me, but because meeting people during this tender window of life creates a kind of honesty and intimacy that rarely exists anywhere else.

When I was fourteen, both of my parents were diagnosed with cancer at the same time. As an only child, my high school years were spent watching my mother, whose illness was more severe, move in and out of hospitals, surgeries, chemotherapy, and radiation. She was a rare and beautiful person: an artist, a lover of food and animals, and a deeply attentive mother until cancer ravaged her life. She died when I was eighteen, and her death flattened me to a shell of the young woman I had been becoming.

Years later, when my father's cancer worsened, I became his caregiver. At twenty-four, I brought him home and cared for him myself. I woke throughout the night to check on him. I emptied his bedpan, scrubbed his dentures, cooked meals, administered medication, and cried more than I thought possible. I had no idea how I was going to survive any of it.

But when the hospice team arrived, everything changed. The nurses, doctor, social worker, and bereavement counselor surrounded my father and me with such care that I finally felt safe again. Because of their support, my father was able to have a peaceful death, and I was able to be there beside him in the way we both needed.

Being able to offer that same kind of peace and support to others became its own form of healing along my journey through loss.

And it was that experience that allowed me to walk into Ron and Ken's apartment that first day and understand what Ron was carrying. It allowed me to sit fearlessly on the edge of Ken's bed and talk with him. It allowed me to recognize the beauty and intimacy of what they were living through in those final weeks together.

I do not say this to diminish the fear, sadness, and pain that filled that apartment. Those emotions were present, of course. But so were laughter, tenderness, and an extraordinary devotion between two people who loved each other deeply. Life and beauty and fear and death coexist more often than we realize. To witness such moments is a profound privilege.

In the weeks before Ken died, I spent more time talking

with him than with Ron. I knew that my relationship with Ron would continue after Ken was gone, so I focused on the time I had getting to know Ken. He was truly an extraordinary person.

Ken had been dealing with cancer for much of his life, but instead of letting it shrink his world, he seemed to command the opposite. Cancer had taught him to embrace life fully. He loved deeply, laughed easily, and approached the world with a kind of mischievous curiosity and childlike wonder that was impossible not to admire. Even when I met him in his most weakened state, he carried a spark that filled the room.

The conversations we had will stay with me for the rest of my life.

A frequent topic of those conversations was Ron. We both worried about him. A self-described "gentle giant," I could feel his loving presence just outside the room where Ken rested. It was clear to me even then that the bond between these two men was extraordinary. The kind of love they shared is something most people spend a lifetime hoping to find.

Some of Ken's last words to me were about Ron. I wrote them down and promised Ken that I would check in on Ron and do my best to make sure he would be okay.

I knew Ron's grief would be vast. But I also knew that love like theirs does not disappear. It transforms. It becomes something that continues to shape the life of the one who remains.

Reading the pages of the book you are about to enter, you will see that Ron found his way through that grief. Not by escaping it, but by allowing it to deepen his understanding of love, loss, and what it means to keep living after everything changes.

Not everyone who survives a caregiving experience and the death of a beloved partner is able to let grief open them into a life of deeper meaning. Ron did.

This book is a testament to the enduring power of love, and to the ways loss, painful as it is, can still deliver its own unexpected gifts.

WHY I WROTE THIS

I've always written my way through life. It's just how I process the world—pen first, feelings later. It has felt natural since I first held a blue Pilot ballpoint pen in my hand and began scrawling on an old yellow stenography pad when I was 13.

So, when my husband Ken died, it was inevitable that I would write about it. Not because I decided to make something of the grief, but because it insisted on being translated. Writing was the only language I knew that could hold the immensity of love and loss at the same time.

I'd been a writer long before I was a widower. But after Ken's death, writing changed shape—it stopped being a craft and became a companion. I didn't just write to understand what had happened, I wrote to stay connected to what still was. I wrote to remember the sound of his laugh, the precision of his humor, the feel of a world where he still existed.

In time, the pages filled with more than sorrow. They held wonder, absurdity, gratitude, and the ongoing surprise that life could still be beautiful. I realized that what I was creating wasn't a record of loss—it was a record of living. Writing had done what it always does for me: it turned chaos into coherence, ache into art, and moments into meaning.

This book is the natural evolution of that process. It gathers together essays written over years—stories of love, death, laughter, hope, friendship, and the thousand small ways we remake a life after it's been cracked wide open.

The Luck We Carry isn't about moving on; it's about moving with. It's a reminder that what we survive becomes part of who we are, and that the luck we carry isn't the absence of hardship, but the grace to keep showing up—with humor, with heart, and with pen in hand.

PART I: THE CLIMB

LOVE ASKS US TO RISE. LOSS ASKS US TO KEEP CLIMBING

THE MEET CUTE

My breath trailed behind me like steam from a locomotive as I walked the two blocks to a little neighborhood bar on a frigid March night. I'd loved this part of Chicago's North Side since moving from the chaos of Boystown a couple of years earlier. It was quieter, more residential, and held a surprise I hadn't expected.

I'd spotted the rainbow flag above the bar entrance a few times when getting off the "L." I finally looked it up on Yahoo! (Google wasn't a thing yet) and confirmed what I suspected: it was a gay bar. Not the loud, sweaty kind I'd grown tired of, but a cozy little place with friendly bartenders, smiling regulars, and pours generous enough to make you stay awhile. Just two blocks from my apartment. Perfection.

It was crowded that night—the kind of crowded that feels like a party you were meant to find. Condensation fogged the windows, laughter ricocheted around the room, and the air smelled like beer and citrus. I snaked through the bodies to the bar, where the bartender slid me a cosmopolitan before I'd even asked. Apparently, he'd paid attention on a previous visit.

As I sipped the cold tartness, I scanned the room—not

looking for anything specific, just people-watching and checking for eye candy. That night, the bold version of me had shown up —the one who moves through the world without apology, the one who had pulled me through my first lonely years in Chicago by forcing me out of my apartment and into life.

That's when I saw him.

At the far end of the bar sat a man with dark, wavy hair and a smile that could power the city grid. He looked familiar, which immediately made my brain do backflips trying to remember where I'd seen him before. My silent sleuthing was interrupted when a guy in an Armani suit on the next barstool spun toward me.

"Hi. I'm Greg. Can I buy you a drink?" he asked, clearly expecting me to say yes.

"I'm Ron. Still working on this one." I gestured to my cosmo. "But thanks."

"I don't get over very often. What's this crowd like?" he asked.

"I don't really know. I haven't been here in a while." I looked past him to see if I could see the handsome guy. Armani guy was probably handsome, too, but I didn't notice.

"Oh yeah? Where do you usually go?"

"My sofa."

He laughed. "That's a shame, Ron."

Great. Armani guy remembered my name, but I had no memory of his. I excused myself to the bathroom, maneuvering through the crowd. The bar was tiny and packed with people. As I serpentined around bodies to get to the bathroom in the back, I found myself face-to-face with the handsome guy I'd seen when I first sat down. He stopped me with a grin and a greeting. "Hi, I'm Ken. We met a couple of months ago." We were standing in close quarters, so I could see the crinkles around his eyes when he smiled.

I remembered instantly—the night, the conversation, the paper. The guy journaling in a bar.

It had been a couple of months earlier on Friday, January 12. I'd seen him sitting alone, scribbling on beautiful paper with a fountain pen. A man who journals—in public? I was hooked. I'd asked what he was writing before boldly sliding the paper toward me to "read." (His handwriting was indecipherable, but that wasn't the point.)

"Just some thoughts," he'd said, smiling.

"You come to a crowded bar to sit here and not talk to anyone?" I asked.

"You're talking to me," he replied, that smile deepening. His eyes seemed to twinkle when he smiled.

We'd hit it off immediately—bonding over improv training (mine at Second City, his at Improv Olympic). We talked, laughed, and connected until a friend pulled me away for drinks, and by the time I returned, Ken was surrounded. I went home furious and half-drunk, leaving the world's most embarrassing voicemail: "I called dibs!"

So now, two months later, fate had corrected itself.

Back at the bar, Armani Guy was still trying. But Ken—playing darts at the other end—had my full attention. When I noticed a drunk admirer pawing at him, he met my gaze and rolled his eyes in return. Butterflies swarmed my stomach as he walked over to me.

"Ugh. That guy won't leave me alone," he said.

I leaned in conspiratorially. "Want me to help?"

"How?"

"Go back to playing. When you need rescuing, tug your ear —like Carol Burnett."

He laughed. "Really?"

"Trust me."

While I waited for "the sign," I slugged back a few more

cocktails and made small talk with Armani; time seemed to stand still. I kept Ken in my peripheral vision while trying to be polite. I glanced over and saw Ken standing in a group by the dartboard where they were playing, tugging his earlobe. It was "go time."

I slithered through the crowd to the back of the bar, where the dart game was happening in true improv style: no plans for what I would say or do. They were all huddled around the dartboard when no one was throwing. I stopped short of the group of them. "What the fuck, Ken?" The crowd between us parted like the Red Sea. My voice was loud, angry, and thrilling. "What are you doing here? You said you were going to the library!"

The crowd fell silent. "Oh—hi, Ronnie," he said, instantly in on the bit.

"That's all you've got? Hi, Ronnie?" I said, hand on my hip.

As he expertly stammered for words, his drunken admirer skulked away, hoping to avoid the improvised drama. "I just stopped in for a little while."

"A little while? It's 10:30! Don't you think I was worried?"

"I'm sorry," he replied so convincingly that I almost felt bad for yelling at him.

"This has been a long time coming. We need to talk." I lurched forward, grabbed his hand and pulled him around the corner, out of sight from our onlookers, who all began to move away. Their night was over. Mine was just beginning.

"You were amazing!" he said, eyes bright. "I owe you a drink."

We settled into two stools in the corner by the jukebox and fell into a time warp. Conversation was effortless. It was as if the universe had been holding its breath, waiting for us to meet properly this time.

"I have a confession," he said. "I've been coming here every Friday since we met in January, hoping to see you again."

"You have?" My heart did somersaults.

He smiled shyly. "I just hope I don't put my foot in my mouth again." Then he reached down, pressed a button seemingly behind his knee, and—click—detached his prosthetic leg, putting the foot near his mouth. "Too late?" he grinned.

I laughed nervously. It was unexpected, to say the least. "I guess that ship has sailed."

"I had cancer when I was fourteen," he said. "I lost my leg below the knee."

I was stunned—not by the fact itself, but by the grace with which he said it. The humor. The complete lack of self-pity. He wasn't defined by what he'd lost. He was lit from within by what he still had.

And I wanted in on that light.

"I have a confession of my own," I said. "I haven't been here since that night because I thought I'd missed out on something special, and I didn't want to be reminded of it." It didn't feel daring to reveal this to him. Whatever pulled us together seemed to be pulling out my feelings, too.

"I'm glad you came here tonight," he said sweetly, holding his beer bottle to toast. I clinked my vodka tonic against it.

We left hand in hand, walking through the cold Chicago night toward my apartment. The air was sharp and bright. Everything shimmered with possibility.

On his fortieth birthday in 2005, I organized a party where guests (near and far) wrote a poem about him in any style of their choosing. There were limericks, haikus, sonnets, and more, all around the topic of Ken and his amazingness. Mine immortalized that night of our first meeting:

I thought I knew what a partner was
But I didn't have a clue
Until one cold winter night in 2001
At a bar, I ran into you

So handsome and so nonchalant
Sitting there in overalls, writing
This man I knew I had to somehow meet
Would he be turned off by my wit, so biting?

I grabbed the piece of paper from you
Composed myself and read
My mind a bit hazy, I handed it back and thought
"I have no idea what it said."

But that was over 4 years ago
This wasn't a passing fling
My life has been an adventure with you
And I wouldn't change a thing

You're an amazing partner, an amazing man
You're all about the journey
Wanting to get to the destination
I certainly wish you'd hurry!

THAT NIGHT in 2001 was our beginning. I didn't know it yet, but it would be the most beautiful story I'd ever live—and the one that would change me forever.

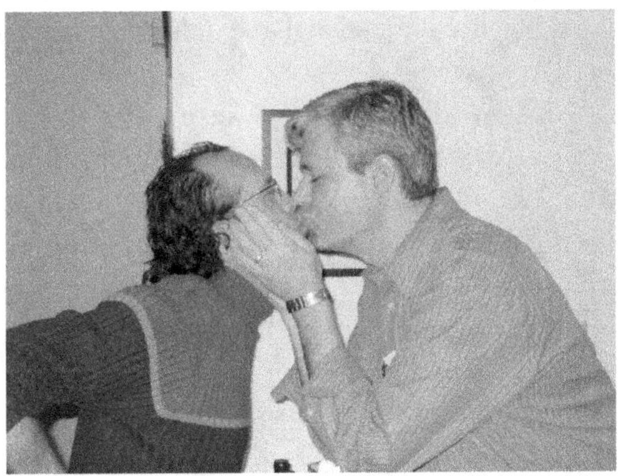

A birthday kiss on his 40th.

Author's Note:

Every great love story starts with a ridiculous moment. No one tells you that the night you meet the love of your life won't feel cinematic at all—it'll feel awkward, funny, and strangely familiar. You won't hear violins or see soft lighting. You'll just feel something quietly shift, as if life tilts a little toward its true north. When I met Ken on a cold Chicago night in 2001, I didn't know he'd become my whole story—or that I'd one day have to learn how to keep writing it without him. But that night, all I knew was this: something extraordinary was beginning in the most ordinary place imaginable—a neighborhood bar, a glass of cheap vodka, and one very good reason to stay for another round.

Looking back, I realize that night was more than a beginning—it was an anchor. Every laugh, every touch, every ordinary Friday that followed would become part of the map I still carry. When you lose someone you love, your memories stop being stories from the past and become coordinates for finding yourself again. The night I met Ken was when I first learned that love doesn't save you—it shapes you. And if you're lucky, it leaves behind a light bright enough to guide you home long after the changes.

When I first wrote this story, I wasn't trying to capture a grand romance. I was just trying to remember what it felt like to begin. After loss, beginnings become sacred things—rare and radiant, like light through glass. Revisiting this story years later, I was struck by how ordinary the night was, and how extraordinary it became. That's how love works. It doesn't announce itself. It just sits down next to you, buys you a drink, and changes your life.

The Meet Cute isn't just how I met Ken—it's how I met myself before I knew I'd need to remember who that was.

A FAMILIAR PAIN

"It's been aching for a while," Ken said.

We were standing in our bright orange-and-yellow kitchen, getting coffee one Thursday morning. We'd painted it not long after moving in a few years earlier. The dining room had a deep red accent wall. One bedroom wall was moss green. All of it was Ken's idea. To say he lived vibrantly would be an understatement.

But as he spoke, the color drained from the room.

"How long?" I asked. I already had a sense, but I needed him to say it. He'd been uncomfortable for a while. That alone wasn't alarming. His pain tolerance was almost superhuman, forged by a lifetime of endurance: an amputation, multiple surgeries, cancer treatments. Pain, for him, was rarely worth mentioning.

"A few weeks. Since I fell."

He didn't look at me. And there was something unfamiliar in his voice. Not something added, but something missing. A flatness. A lack of lift. It was unsettling coming from a man whose voice could be silky or silly or sexy, sometimes all at once.

He'd shown me the bruise from when he lost his balance

stepping up into the dining room. His prosthetic hadn't been fully attached. He went down hard. The bruise on his inner thigh was a deep plum stain, the size of an eggplant.

"It's huge," I said, defaulting to optimism. "I'm not surprised it still hurts. Is it feeling any better?"

I was pouring his coffee, grateful for the small, grounding task. Doing something for him—even something ordinary—felt important. He'd never been good at letting anyone help him. Becoming an amputee so young shaped his independence, his strength, his resolve. Letting me in had taken time. A full year, really. But over the years that followed, he trusted me more than anyone. I was his person. I'd waited a long time to be someone's person.

He hesitated. "No. And I've felt this kind of pain before."

"What do you mean?"

I already knew. I didn't want to hear it. One of my life rules —really, a commandment—had always been: don't ask questions you don't want answered. But he looked worried, so I broke it. There was nothing I wouldn't do for him. Eight years together had proven that, though I didn't yet realize how little we'd actually been tested.

"Cancer," he said. "This is what it felt like last time."

There it was again. Or rather, there it wasn't. No inflection. No rhythm. Just defeat. I'd never heard him like this. Ken had always charged forward with fearlessness and wit. I followed his lead more often than not. But not today. Today, I needed to lead.

"Call Terry," I said. "Make an appointment. Once you see him, you'll feel better."

Terry had been Ken's doctor for years. He'd guided him through his last cancer battle fifteen years earlier. On Ken's recommendation, Terry had become my primary physician, too. We trusted him. I needed to believe this would be enough.

A couple of weeks later, Ken called me at work.

"Hi." That voice again. Small. Defeated.

"Hey, baby. What's shakin'?" I stayed buoyant for both of us.

"Terry wants to see us."

"Did he give you the results?"

"No. That's why he wants to see us. Today."

Of course it was today. Same-day appointments. No details. Every sign was flashing red.

"Okay," I said. "I'll head home. I love you."

"I love you, too." He said it quietly, but it mattered. No matter what we learned later, we had each other.

The doctor's office was five minutes from our apartment. I usually walked to my appointments. Today, we drove. Ken was in too much physical pain—and too much emotional limbo—for anything else.

The office was pale and monochromatic. We were called back almost immediately. That had never happened before. I told myself not to borrow trouble, even as trouble felt like it already knew our names.

Terry knocked and entered differently than usual. No sweeping warmth. No easy smile. He was tentative. Careful. I knew then. Or at least I knew what today would bring.

"Hi, guys," he said, shaking our hands. "How are you doing?"

Ken glanced at me, then answered. "Not too bad. But I guess you'll tell me."

Terry exhaled, half-laughed, and shuffled papers. "Kenny, your MRI showed...something. Because of your scar tissue from radiation, it's not entirely clear. But I spoke with two oncologists. Based on your history, we can't imagine it's anything but cancer."

There it was: the words I've dreaded hearing since I fell in love with him eight years ago. Potential words that—for a split second—almost kept me from pursuing a relationship with him. *See? I told you. I warned you about this. You are such an idiot. What are you going to do now? This is it.*

"I knew it," Ken said, glancing over at me. "I knew it," he said again to himself.

"Often, what happens when treating cancer with radiation is a mutation. It's a known potential side effect. The benefit is, of course, that it stopped the tumor's growth fifteen years ago, and you've seen no other incursions—which is good."

"Until now," Ken quipped. "What's next?" Ken asked. I don't think he was interested in a history lesson. It was the future that held his focus.

"I've scheduled you to see an oncologist and an oncological surgeon next week. They are both top in their fields and can help assess the next steps. Of course, I'll be in the loop and here for you whenever you have questions. I know this isn't the news we were hoping for."

"No," Ken replied. His voice started to sound a little more like what I was used to. "No, but I always knew it was a possibility. We'll just have to deal with it." There he was. That was my Ken. The pragmatic fighter.

"Of course we will," Terry replied. "The good news...ironically...is that you've been here before. You know what to expect. It's an advantage most people don't have—if you can call it that."

"That's me. Mr. Lucky," Ken quipped, using his range to make it sound funny.

It was almost like once Ken realized what he was dealing with, he knew the lay of the battlefield and felt comfortable knowing this enemy—one he'd faced and defeated before. He was tense, but there was a kind of relief in knowing what it was, that his feelings about it were right.

Terry turned to me. "How are you doing?" he said kindly.

Me? I had no idea how I was doing. I'd just heard the news no one wants to hear about someone they love. "I'm fine," I replied robotically. Of course, I was fine. I didn't have cancer. "I'm in shock, but I'll do anything to support Ken." I turned to Ken. "We'll get through this together." I wasn't sure what to say. But I knew it was clear this wasn't about me, and I'd focus all my efforts on helping him deal with this diagnosis and beat it—if that were possible.

He smiled and squeezed my hand. "Together."

"Kenny," Terry began, "I know it's also bad news that you've been here before, unfortunately. But you're young and strong, and I have complete faith in our oncologists. I have the appointment information for you. But besides the medical aspect, do you feel like you have a support system in place to help you through this?"

"Yes," he replied immediately. His voice continued its return to his old way of speaking. Maybe it was the uncertainty of what was to come that muted him. In this very odd, very heavy moment, I could feel him returning to me, returning to fight. "I have Ronnie. And my family and friends. And... Ronnie." He said it again calmly and confidently. He was my person, and I was his.

Most importantly, he was correct. Ken knew he had me. I was grateful for that. I'd certainly be grateful for his support if the situation were reversed. I just needed to make sure I came through for him. I would take on anything to support him. Because not having him in my life wasn't an option I'd even consider.

"Again, fellas, I'm sorry to report this news to you. I hope you can still have a nice Thanksgiving." We all stood up and shook hands. I'd completely forgotten it was Thanksgiving week.

Falling in love with Ken had been easy. Remaining in love

with him—even easier. However, regarding myself as his primary support system was both an honor and a daunting, weighty task. I felt like I was standing on an empty beach, looking out to sea at a massive tsunami, gaining momentum, height, and power as it approached the shore. I was the only thing standing between it and Ken. It towered over me, casting an ominous shadow that felt cold. I didn't know what to expect or what it would do. I knew I would stand firm and fight for him with everything I had. I hoped it would be enough.

We left the doctor's office hand in hand to face whatever was to come. But first, there would be martinis.

Martinis marked special occasions for us: both good and troubling.

Author's Note:

This essay captures the moment when fear stopped being hypothetical. When you love someone who has already survived the unimaginable, you convince yourself there must be a limit. A cap. A lifetime maximum. Surely one person can't be asked to endure the same battle again. Surely love counts for something. Surely the universe keeps score.

It doesn't.

What this moment taught me—though I didn't fully understand it yet—was that love doesn't protect you from hard things. It positions you inside them. Front row. No armor. No escape hatch. Just presence.

I didn't know how the story would unfold when we left Terry's office that day. I only knew who I was to Ken. And who he was to me. That knowledge didn't make the road easier, but it made it clear.

This essay lives early in the book because it marks a quiet shift. From falling in love to choosing it. From romance to responsibility. From optimism to resolve. And yes—there really were martinis. Some rituals don't fix anything. They just help you take the next step.

IT'S 3:12 A.M. AND ALL IS DEFINITELY NOT WELL

I pulled up to the cancer center, settled Ken into his wheelchair, and wheeled him inside. While a nurse guided him to radiation, I sprinted upstairs to tell his favorite nurse, Blanca, he'd be up soon for transfusion number two. The last one had worked wonders—color in his face, energy in his voice. We were hoping for another lift.

"How's he doing?" Blanca asked, pausing mid-task, all warmth and focus. She'd been a gift from the start—kind, quick-witted, steady. She loved Ken's spirit, grace, and style. When Ken showed up for infusion with a printed label over his port that read "You're So Vein," she laughed so hard, she doubled over. She loved the light he brought into that room. And, he brought it everywhere.

"Better," I said. "Feeling good enough to flirt shamelessly with you I would imagine." We'd all referred to this incredible woman as "Kenny's Girlfriend" since the very first infusion. She loved playing with him. Whenever Ken was around—even while receiving toxic chemicals into his body—there was always laughter.

She laughed. "Good. I'm ready."

Radiation usually took fifteen minutes—less time than it took me to park. But before I reached the waiting area downstairs, a nurse rushed past. "You can go in. He's having trouble breathing."

I rushed into the room and found Ken sitting upright on the table. He was wearing an oxygen mask, tethered to a large green tank on wheels. His breathing was labored, but—as usual—he was calm.

"I couldn't breathe," he said between shallow puffs behind the clear plastic mask. "Like at home when I'm anxious." He was wearing a faded Disney World beanie he'd gotten when his family visited there when he was a little boy. Faded yellow and blue with a picture of Mickey, Minnie, Daffy, and Pluto embroidered on each of the four triangles that comprised it. He took comfort in nostalgia, and physically having something from his past seemed to soothe him—maybe anchored him—in a particular place in his life, like his carefree childhood before cancer arrived and took all of that away.

"So, this has happened before?" the on-duty oncologist, Dr. Chung, asked. His regular radiation oncologist wasn't there that day, so he was being attended to by the "glamorous Dr. Chung," as we called her (even to her face). We'd seen her before in our regular doctor's absence. She was always impeccably made up and wore fashion-forward outfits, usually paired with kicky boots that we inevitably commented on. She was sweet, always smiling, but knew her stuff. We knew we were in good hands.

"Sometimes at night," I said. Anxiety? Progression? Our enemy was everywhere. Shore up one system, and another buckled.

"I want to take you guys across the street to the ER to get Kenny checked out," she said, directing an orderly to bring his wheelchair over to the table where he sat.

I tucked a blanket around Ken against the March cold and

pushed, Dr. Chung behind us, rolling the oxygen tank in three-inch leather boots. Abbey Road: wheelchair, oxygen, terrified husband, kicky boots. We arrived at 2 p.m. He was triaged, X-rayed, scanned, bled. We waited. At 7:30 p.m., finally, an ER room. At 11 p.m., admitted. At 2 a.m., a hospital bed. Twelve hours since we'd walked in.

He was so tired, squirming with discomfort as we waited, but his humor and sense of gratitude never left him. We sat in the waiting room, people watching and making jokes like we were sitting in an airport bound for Bora Bora. He made time with him feel like home, no matter what he was feeling.

They weighed him in a sling as they lifted him from the gurney to the long-awaited bed. Double digits. Ninety-something pounds. So small. How had I not seen it before? How had all of this snowballed into something that felt so uncontrollable? Insurmountable.

"Go home, vavy," he murmured, sedated and spent. "You're tired." Even now, he worried about me.

"I'll go when you're asleep. Until then, I'm here. I like you, remember?" I kissed his forehead.

"Oh yeah, you do." A drowsy smile. "And you don't like that many people."

"Exactly. You're special."

He sighed and drifted off to wherever exhaustion and sleeping meds would take him. I sat another hour, trying to hold the present still while the past slipped away and the future loomed, unwanted. I wished the silence could freeze time long enough for me to catch up. It never did.

At 3 a.m., he slept. I needed rest to be useful in the morning. I'd come without a jacket, thinking we'd be in and out of radiation and the transfusion. The walk to the parking garage stung. At the top level, our Prius sat nearly alone. I slid into the ice-cold driver's seat and stared at the clock.

3:12 a.m.

Is this it? The beginning of the end? Will he come home? Sitting alone in that cold car felt like a preview of what was coming: me, alone with decisions, an empty seat beside me. A small, quiet moment that roared.

I snapped a photo of the clock because I didn't want to forget the feeling—the gravity, the pivot. A before and an after. Today had made something plain: there would be no montage, no neat resolution. Only fighting—fiercely—for Ken, for time, for whatever hours we could steal.

Back home, I stayed up as late as I could, journaling, trying to pin the day to the page—to keep today here, to hold tomorrow at bay. Tomorrows were fog now, and somewhere ahead waited one that wouldn't include him. I wasn't ready for it. I never would be.

But at 3:12 a.m., I knew this much: morning was coming, whether I wanted it or not—and I would meet it beside him, for as long as I still could.

An unforgettable moment in my life.

Author's Note:

This is the night I knew. Not because a doctor said so, but because something inside me did. There's a particular kind of knowing that seeps in quietly, long before your heart is ready to hear it.

Looking back, this was the pivot—the moment when caregiving turned into goodbye. What strikes me most now isn't the panic or exhaustion, but the stillness. Grief doesn't always arrive with thunder. Sometimes it shows up as a clock glowing in the dark, a photo you take to mark the second your world shifts.

At 3:12 a.m., I began to understand what it meant to live inside the in-between—the space where love keeps you moving even as loss begins to settle in. This essay is about that moment. The one where you stop asking if the end is coming and start whispering to yourself, not yet.

PLANNING THE SOIRÉE OF A LIFETIME

My therapist, Andrea, suggested I talk with Ken about his funeral. "Involve him in it," she said. "You two talk about everything else—why not this? He'll feel some control over something as personal as this. And knowing Ken, he'll have ideas that make it uniquely his."

"It wouldn't be weird? Or selfish?"

"Not at all," she said. "Just ask if he'd like to be involved. If so, you plan together. If not, you handle it however you want." She smiled. "But I have a feeling he'll want in."

She was right. Andrea, the cancer center's social worker, had known Ken for only a short time, but his big presence made him easy to read. We'd met her early in his treatment rounds but hadn't really talked until his cancer returned. When it did, I knew I needed help finding the tools to support him—and survive it myself.

It took me a week to bring it up. There were so many quiet nights when I almost did—after visitors left, after his parents went home, after the day settled into the kind of stillness that made everything feel suspended. But I couldn't. He'd been slipping away, piece by piece, and when we found our way to a moment of calm, I wanted to stay in it.

Then my best friend Kathy called.

"I have an idea," she said. "Call me crazy, but what if you have the memorial at a theater? Ken's a performer—it would be *so* him."

"Oh my god, yes." The idea landed like light through fog.

"Remember that place on Halsted where he did his one-man show? They know him there, right?"

"That's perfect," I said. "Thank you." It felt strange to be excited about finding the perfect event for your 45-year-old husband's memorial. But, in hospice, the rules are just different. It was exactly the kind of idea that would have excited him—and for the first time, I felt a flicker of excitement too.

"Do you have time for a chat?" I asked later that day when I finally summoned the courage for this kind of discussion.

"Sure, vavy. Pull up a chair." He was in good spirits and feeling fine, lying in the hospital bed in the living room. His parents were taking a break that day, and we had a good couple of hours before our friends Tina and Bruce stopped by with dinner.

"I wanted to talk about your...memorial." I couldn't say funeral. "Is it something...would you want to be involved in planning it?"

His eyes brightened. "Oh, yes. I would love that." He used his leg to push himself up in bed. "I've actually been thinking about it and wanted to talk to you."

"You have?"

"Well, I have a lot of time to think about things, ya know?" He smiled.

"Well, okay, good." I brought a pad and a pen to make notes. "So, what ya got? Hit me with your best shot."

"I want a soirée," he stated adamantly. His face was very

serious. "Not a funeral. Not a memorial. A soirée. A party. Friends. Laughter. Community. A soirée."

"A soirée it is," I said, writing it down. His enthusiasm steadied me. "I was thinking we could bring some of your artwork to display at the theater."

"Oh, yeah, vavy, I love that." His eyes softened. And I always loved it when he called me his stylized version of "baby," as he had since the beginning of our relationship.

"Then we can pick which ones later."

"Now," he said, swinging his legs to the side of the bed. Ken never waited for anything—not even death. He was still the "body in motion" I fell in love with ten years before.

I helped him into his wheelchair, and we rolled through the apartment, revisiting the art that made up his creative finger-print: the nine-piece installation of street sweeper brushes, his raffia-wrapped gifts adorned with Scrabble tiles, the color-coded lint collages he'd once made from the dryer. He was delighted, energized, alive in the act of creating again—even if what we were creating was a farewell. When we'd finished, I collapsed on the couch across from him, now back in bed.

"This feels weird, doesn't it?" It came out before I knew if it was something I should have said.

"It's weird that I won't be there," he said quietly.

"I know," I said, barely audible. "But you will be. Your art will fill the room. You will."

He nodded but didn't look convinced. I think he was disap-pointed to miss such a great party. We'd been a party planning team since the beginning. Our annual Christmas party was legendary, and we stuffed our apartment with friends from across the city and suburbs.

After a moment, he looked outside. "It's nice out. Let's go into the backyard and have a tini."

He was right. And a martini sounded perfect after such a

heavy conversation. I bundled him in a blanket, hooked up his oxygen, and wheeled him to the garden he'd tended for years. Early spring had just begun to blush through the soil—tiny signs of life returning. I shook the martinis and joined him.

When I came back, he was quiet, lost in thought. His face had grown pale, his frame small. He was disappearing before my eyes, and yet, sitting there, he was more him than ever—funny, elegant, endlessly himself.

"What're you thinking about?" I asked.

He didn't answer right away. "What am I thinking about?" he echoed, half to himself. His voice was softer these days, his words sometimes far away. Then he turned to me. "I'm thinking that a discourse on one's demise is fucking exhausting."

We laughed, loud and real. Humor was still our native language. Even now, Ken wasn't a victim of cancer; he was directing the final act of his life with wit and grace. It wasn't just a plan for his memorial—it was another collaboration, another story we were building together. A final production. A soirée.

And as always, he knew how to end a scene.

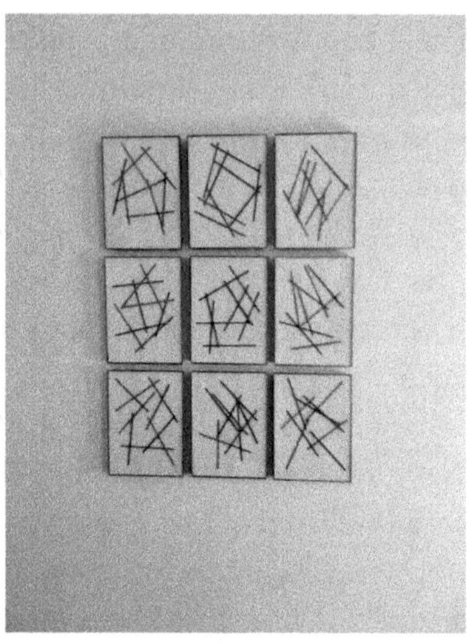

Ken's artistic eye saw art in street sweeper bristles
he found over the years.

Author's Note:

Looking back, this was the moment I realized grief could be creative. Ken's soirée wasn't about denying death—it was about staging one last act together. We'd spent our lives collaborating —on art, on parties, on laughter—and now, somehow, we were collaborating on goodbye. The absurdity of that still makes me smile. But in the middle of all that pain, it was oddly comforting to plan something that looked like us.

What I didn't understand then was that this would be my first lesson in the alchemy of mourning: how grief can become art, how loss can still hold color. That day, in our apartment, full of laughter and lists, we were building something beautiful from the unbearable.

The soirée became both his farewell and my beginning—the first time I saw that storytelling could be a form of survival.

THE LAST DAY ON THE FIRST

We have another bathroom, I thought, when my brother-in-law, Craig, rapped on the door. Moments of privacy in a house full of well-meaning guests were rare. For nine surreal weeks, my husband, Ken, had rested in a hospital bed in our front room after being released into home hospice care for what would be the final chapter of his life.

"You should hurry up," Craig said, his voice low, urgent.

It took a moment to register. Then I bolted down the hall to kneel beside Ken, gently holding his pale, spidery hand.

It had been a long night. Ken had grown less responsive over the past week—sleeping more, eating less. His mom, Mama Jo, had flown back from California when I'd sounded "the alarm." My best friend, Kathy, and his best friend, Kim, rounded out the vigil—along with so many others who'd passed through in recent weeks.

The night before, he'd been restless and incoherent, just as the hospice nurses warned he might be. Around 3 a.m., I heard movement from the front room. Kim and my mother-in-law were dabbing his forehead with a damp cloth. His body was twitching as it began to shut down. The nurses had assured me he wasn't in pain, but it was devastating to watch. The once-vibrant, creative man I loved—just forty-five—had become a fragile shadow. Part of me was relieved to see this cruel part of the journey nearing its end. I was grateful—envious, even—that he no longer seemed aware of what was happening.

We'd called Craig the day before and told him to come as soon as possible. His red-eye from Los Angeles was due at 7:30 a.m. I didn't know how long Ken would last. Judging by his glassy eyes and uneven breathing, I doubted it would be long.

I was running on fumes—little sleep, frayed nerves, a fractured heart. Still, something stronger pulled me through: our connection, our love, my duty to stay with him to the end. By 3:30 a.m., I was on my second soup-bowl-sized mug of coffee. The rest of the house began to stir. Incredibly, there was laughter among the grief—small, defiant bursts of life.

During those weeks of hospice, I'd become adept at staying in the moment. Ken's love of life was legendary; his resilience unmatched. A part of me still half-believed he could rally again, though I knew better. For months, I'd refused to imagine a world without him. But that morning—June 1, 2011—the world was preparing to show me otherwise.

We'd said everything that needed saying. Through tears and trembling, we told each other—more than once—how much we loved each other, how impossible it was to let go. There were no regrets. I paged the hospice nurse, hoping she could come, but she was with another family who needed her as much as we did. There was nothing to do but make him comfortable, hold him close, and wait.

As the sun rose into a cloudless sky, Kim tracked Craig's progress from O'Hare to our apartment on Chicago's North Side. She went to meet him, determined to get him to Ken as quickly as possible. Everyone was laser-focused on Ken and what this day might bring for us.

Craig had arrived around nine, went straight to Ken's bedside, and took his hand—loving him for himself, for his wife, for their sons. Twenty minutes later, Ken died. I was beside him, whispering love into his ear, wishing him well on his next adventure. I was grateful Craig made it in time. I'm certain Ken waited for him. They were close, and it was just like Ken—thoughtful, gallant—to hold on until he knew I'd have someone to lean on. Even cancer couldn't take that from him.

After the devastation came relief. Relief that he wasn't suffering. Relief that the relentless rhythm of caregiving had ended. That sounds callous, but it was real. I had pushed myself mercilessly—because I could, because I loved him—and because I knew the time to rest would come. That time had arrived.

The rest of that day comes to me in flashes and still frames. It was over. Craig handled what he could; Kim stayed with Ken's body when the funeral home came. I couldn't bear to watch them carry him out. It may have been just a shell, but it was one I loved—his wavy brown hair, the freckle on his cheek, the scar from surgery.

By mid-afternoon, everyone had gone except Craig and Mama Jo. We sat in the backyard, and thanks to Craig's steady hand, my martini glass was never empty. It was, impossibly, a gorgeous day—bright, breezy, golden. I remember thinking, even in that grief, that it was the most beautiful day of that summer.

Maybe because it had to be.

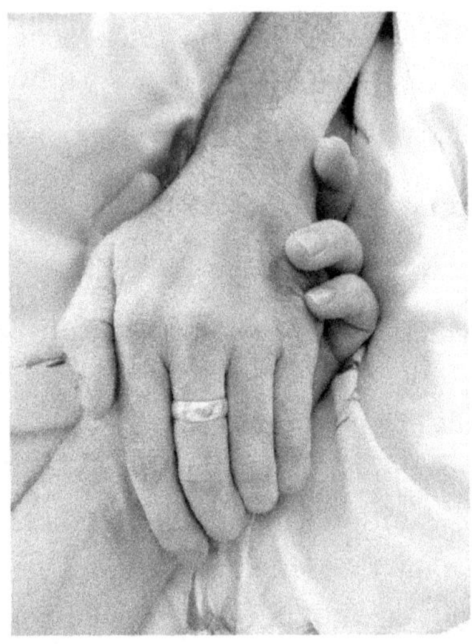

I snapped this pic the day before he died. I never
wanted to forget his hand (on top)—or how
perfectly it fit into mine.

AUTHOR'S NOTE:

This was the day everything stopped—and began again.

I used to think of June 1, 2011, as the day my story ended. For a long time, I couldn't see past it. But with time and distance, I've come to understand it differently. This was the day love took on a new form—quieter, invisible, but no less real.

I remember the stillness of that morning more than the pain. The way light poured through the windows. The way the world kept turning, even as mine fell apart. There was something holy about it, something beyond comprehension. Maybe that's what grace looks like—showing up in the middle of heartbreak, uninvited but insistent.

Writing about this day was harder than reliving it. The act

of putting it into words made it real in a way that memory never could. But it also reminded me that bearing witness is part of love, too.

MOUNTAIN CLIMBING FOR BEGINNERS

When my husband, Ken, was diagnosed with terminal cancer, I began a climb I didn't know existed—and there was no way around it. It was unexpected, brutal, and often felt impossible. But I climbed because I had no choice. With no time to plan, I grabbed onto whatever I could—even a pinprick of rock outcropping—and endured the emotional cuts and bruises because I had to be with him. To support him. To love him. Until he no longer needed me. Until he was free from suffering. I would be his escort, guardian, and protector—no one else. Though helping hands were often offered along the way, I usually swatted them away. I needed to make this climb with him. Alone. Together.

It was only a few days before Thanksgiving when Ken's doctor told us the cancer had returned. The ground shifted beneath me. At first, it seemed like a hill we might manage, but as remedies failed and hope grew thinner, the slope rose higher until it disappeared into clouds. I couldn't see the top anymore—only the long, dark path ahead.

I wasn't equipped for this kind of climb, but there was no turning back. Ken and I had spent ten years building the kind of partnership I'd always dreamed of—equal parts love, laughter, and shared creativity. He was my rock, my cheerleader, my home. And when the person you rely on most begins to slip away, instinct takes over. You climb because you must.

We'd faced smaller mountains before—his earlier injuries, surgeries, recoveries. But this one was different. This one had no return trail. We'd start together, but only I would come home. Alone. Changed.

So I learned to climb by climbing. I stopped measuring time in months or milestones and focused instead on seconds—the tiny, sacred moments that fill your lungs when you're gasping for air. A smile. A shared laugh. A perfect bloom in the hospital garden. Gratitude lived in the smallest cracks of light.

Grief was always there on the mountain, lurking in the periphery. An interloper. An echo. I hated him, raged against him, cursed him on the pages of my journal. I swore he wouldn't win. But somewhere deep down, I knew fighting grief was like fighting gravity.

I'd seen enough '70s television to know a few things about quicksand. It showed up often enough to make me believe adulthood would be full of it. The secret, I'd learned, was not to struggle—struggling just made you sink faster. Turns out grief works the same way.

Eventually, I stopped fighting. I became transparent in my sorrow, letting it move through me instead of against me. If grief couldn't catch on anything, maybe it couldn't consume me. Acceptance became my invisibility cloak. I focused entirely on Ken, refusing to waste what was left of his time dreading the years I'd face without him.

In the final nine weeks, when our home became a hospice, I found a peace I never expected. Despite the obstacles, there was laughter. There was light. There was grace—his and, somehow, mine. Ken led us through it all with humor and dignity, like he already knew the way to the summit.

At night, after he fell asleep, I wrote. I wrote to steady myself, to understand the swirl of thoughts that chased me through the dark. Those quiet hours were my rope line—my connection to something larger than my pain. When I cast my fear into words, it came back to me as calm.

The last days were the steepest. Ken's body grew small, his voice quiet, his spirit already halfway to the other side. On the final ascent, I carried him. And when we reached the summit—when he took his final breath—there was a single moment of blinding clarity. The air was thin, pure. Everything made sense. Then it was gone.

And I was left to make the descent. Alone.

Grief offered me his hand. This time, I took it.

He guided me down the mountain with an unexpected tenderness. Sometimes, it would overwhelm me so I couldn't fixate on any one feeling, and sometimes it would numb me just enough to function. Grief is a shapeshifter—both a destroyer and protector. It dulled the sharp edges of pain so I could keep moving.

As I descended, I began to see how grief could fill an empty room or make a crowded one feel hollow. It demanded my attention, but it also gave me permission—to rest, to rage, to weep, to laugh again when laughter returned. Grief, it turned out, wasn't my enemy. It was my companion on the way home.

Eventually, the landscape flattened. I turned to look back and saw not devastation, but beauty. Reverence. Every bruise, every misstep, every act of love etched into that mountain's face. I learned that Ken and I had been exactly who we thought we were to each other—right to the end. I showed up every day, in every way I could, until he drew his last breath. That was the greatest gift I could ever give. And it changed me forever.

I've climbed other mountains of grief since—when my father died, when life demanded it—but none as steep, as punishing, or as sacred as the one I climbed with Ken. The second time, the path wasn't vertical. It was familiar. Walkable. I knew how to steady those around me because I had been there before.

Because now, I am a mountain climber.

Ken led us on the climb with courage, humor, and grace.

Author's Note:

This essay marks the turning point in my story—the moment when love and loss become one climb. When Ken was dying, I thought I was learning how to let go. What I was really learning was how to hold on differently.

I didn't set out to write a metaphor about mountains; it revealed itself in the retelling. That's what grief does—it offers new language for the unspeakable. Each step of this story was one I actually took: the resistance, the exhaustion, the surrender, the small, ordinary joys that saved me.

I used to think the climb ended when Ken died. But I've learned that grief keeps reshaping the path—it teaches, protects, and transforms. This was the essay that helped me stop asking when the mountain would end and start realizing: the view changes because I keep climbing.

This essay closes the first act of my grief—the climb, the collapse, the silence that follows—and opens the long, uneven descent toward what comes next: learning how to live with what remains.

PART II: THE DESCENT

GRIEF IS NOT FALLING—IT'S LEARNING HOW TO LAND

A LETTER FROM THE FUTURE

I wrote this letter to myself on March 24, 2011—one day after my tenth anniversary with Ken and the week he was in the hospital before coming home for hospice care, where he would die on June 1. It was the week we learned, definitively, that the cancer had returned and nothing could stop it. All I could do was figure out a way to live in my skin, knowing what was coming and do everything I could to make sure he felt loved until the day he died.

The hospital felt like a world with its own gravity. Everything was slow and heavy. Machines echoed in the background like a dull choir. The fluorescent lights made Ken's skin look too pale, and the antiseptic smell clung to my clothes no matter how long I stood near the window trying to breathe in real air. It was mind-blowing and mind-numbing all at once. I wanted desperately to take care of him the way he had always taken care of me, even though I couldn't see any light ahead. I felt untethered. Lost. Since my present was unbearable, I borrowed strength from the only place I could imagine it existed: the future.

Ken was loved—deeply—by so many that he was never at a loss for visitors. Friends and well-wishers who wanted to spend time with him and show him how much they loved him. It was a great comfort to me in a couple of ways: for Ken's sake, but also for me, so I could check out and be free with my thoughts—for better or worse.

Sitting by the hospital window while Ken entertained guests, I slipped out of that gray March afternoon and wrote to myself from a brighter day that I couldn't yet see. The sky outside was a flat sheet of pewter, the kind that makes you feel like the day is pressing against the glass. Inside, the heat blasted too high, making my neck sweat under my shirt collar. I kept glancing over at him—laughing, telling stories, being the version of himself he fought so naturally to remain—while my hands shook over the page. It felt like I was trying to build a bridge out of paper because in so many ways, I was.

Dear Past Me:

I'm writing to you from the future to give you some vital information. I've inserted this important message in your diary because I —better than anyone—know how integral it is to your mental well-being. The need to write—even during times of crisis—hasn't waned as I'm writing to you.

What you might find shocking is I'm writing from a time when I am content—happy, even. My life is full of love, friendship and creativity. I'm at a point in your life you can't see yet. Just because you can't see it doesn't mean it won't happen. Maybe you think it's not important to see that right now, anyway. You're right. That's part of the reason for this missive.

You are experiencing something very difficult and painful. Take it in. Like sinking in quicksand, fighting it can sometimes pull you deeper in. Relax when you can and let it envelop you. It's only by fully accepting, experiencing and sharing this time in your life that you will best be able to handle it. Make no mistake, though this is one of the darkest times anyone could face, it will not break you. You are stronger than you realize and even more so after this experience. People will wonder how you were able to handle an impossible situation with such grace and dignity. You will astound them, actually. So, prepare for the kindness, compliments and sentiments of love from those around you.

Speaking of friends, you'll remain friends with these amazing people—well into the future. You'll continue to feel a great sense of pride as your friends continue to "circle the wagons" and protect you at all costs. There won't be many surprises, as the friends you love continually come through for you, support you, and love you—and even carry you when necessary. They have done right by you in our past, your present, and in the future. Your taste in friends is flawless, but we already know this, don't we?

Focus your energies on staying healthy so you can continue to love and support your amazing husband. When I think of him now, a smile overtakes my face as I recall our life together. I feel no sadness when I think of him. Only joy and gratitude that he touched my life, and, as you are well aware, changed it and us—for the better. I hope that is of comfort to you. (I guess I already know the answer to that question, don't I?) I chuckle when I think of "body in motion," or "journey vs. destination," or "what if...vs. why not?" The lessons he taught us are still with me. He is only gone in one respect, but ever present in so many more.

You may not consider yourself to be a fighter, but if that's the case, then you are the only one who thinks that. You are strong and graceful. Take care and try to remember these two things well: 1) you are badass, and 2) you will know happiness again.

Future You

During those nine weeks of hospice, I read the letter over and over—out loud, in my office, in the dark. Sometimes I'd sit cross-legged on the floor with my back against the wall, the room lit only by the glow of my computer screen. I could hear the house settling around me, the quiet creaks and taps that reminded me I was alone. My voice would crack halfway through, every time, like my body remembered what my mind wanted to forget. It wrecked me, but it also steadied me. It gave me something to grip when everything else felt like water.

After Ken died, I promised myself that when I could read it without falling apart, I'd share it, hoping it would help others with some creative self-care—because this is what I know now: writing is not just expression—it's survival.

When I read it now, it feels like opening a gift I forgot I'd been given—a message waiting on the other side of the storm. Sometimes, when I read it, I can almost hear the sounds of that hospital room in the background, as if the memory comes with its own soundtrack.

I may not be standing exactly where Future Me promised I'd be, but I'm close. And that's enough.

A sampling of my journals. Journaling saved
my sanity during the difficult times.

Author's Note:

This letter was the first time I realized writing could time travel. It wasn't just me recording grief—it was me sending hope ahead, like a message in a bottle, trusting that one day I'd find it again on a calmer shore. Writing became the only way I could talk to both versions of myself: the one drowning in loss, and the one who would eventually learn to float.

When I wrote this letter, I didn't believe a word of it. But I wrote it anyway. And that act—the willingness to imagine healing before it existed—became its own kind of faith. Grief didn't disappear, but it changed shape. It became a companion instead of a captor. And in that shift, writing became more than therapy—it became a map.

Each time I return to this letter, I'm reminded that even in our darkest moments, some part of us is already reaching toward the light, whispering: Keep going. You're not done yet.

LOST AND FOUND

Dear Ken,

It's June 1, 2021.

I've thought about this day for a long time—what it would feel like to have been without you for as long as I had you. Ten years. How much would it hurt? And what would it mean? Anything? Everything?

I remember the five-year mark in 2016, already anticipating this one. Worrying that it would somehow take something away from me (you know I've always been a pre-worrier). The dread I've felt for this date has abated over the years—each year hurting a little less—though there are sometimes surprise gut punches, reminding me of what was taken from me. But this one feels different. How? I'm not exactly sure. At ten years out, our life together looks like an ornately decorated package that sits on a shelf only to be admired, never opened. We had ten incredible years together. So much love, adventure, and laughter. It hardly seems possible that you've been gone ten more—that our love began two decades—a lifetime ago, really.

It's equally hard to believe I am not the same man who met you in 2001 or said goodbye to you in 2011. I'm still an optimistic, goofy, dog-loving fool. But I think something innately changes in someone who cares for the person he loves most in the world until he takes his last breath. It's inescapable. Boundaries shift. Life itself is redefined without explanation—implicitly. The rules change, and only those of us who have been through it understand. I don't suffer fools gladly and have no patience for self-pity. I think I've taken on many of your traits, though certainly you wore them better. I often wonder what changes you'd notice in me.

Some surprising news: I moved to the suburbs. I sold the loft and bought a little Mid-Century Modern house with a yard—plenty of space for gardening and mowing, and for my Chow Chow, Kallie, to play. Though I was already growing uneasy amid the city's constant hubbub, the pandemic made me crave quiet and space to breathe. You'd love it here. I'm sure you'd love the space, the patio, and the yard. I never thought I'd become a suburbanite until I became one.

While unpacking when I moved in, I found the *It's a Wonderful Life* book I gave you for your birthday in 2002—our first one together. Inside, I'd written "The title of this book is indicative of my life with you." It struck me that I'd signed it, "Always, Ron," instead of "Love, Ron." It seems odd to me that I would have written it that way then, but it feels perfect now. Because "always" has proved true. My love for you hasn't faded—it's only changed form, maybe even grown stronger.

I ended a relationship just before moving into the house—my first serious one since you. It was really easy to fall in love with him—a term I don't throw around casually. He was kind, funny, and loved Ani DiFranco as much as you did. Like you, he was silly, goofy and performed as many funny characters as you did. He was a loving dog dad to his two sweet pups, just as you were to our Chow Chow, Quantum. What can I say? I have a type. I'm drawn to characters. I didn't really notice the similarities at the time, but they've become crystal clear when I look back. Though it didn't work out, it reminded me I'm still capable of that kind of love. It felt good—right—to be loved like that again. You would've liked him. We still text and talk on occasion. It's so like me to continue a relationship with someone who is no longer present in my everyday life.

You'd be happy with how far I've come. You'd have loved the loft where I lived for seven years after I moved out of the apartment we shared. It wasn't as hard to leave as I thought it would be—especially after living there for almost three years after you died. I was ready.

You'd be proud of the life I've built. Now, in my little house, with a close-knit circle of friends and neighbors. You'd love that I've returned to camping—and amused that I still use the same percolator—the one Kathy gave us after our camping trip with her in Ojai. I think of you every time I make that first piping hot pot of coffee in the morning after a night sleeping in our tent, on our air mattress, in our sleeping bag.

I wondered how it would feel to have lost you for as long as I had you. The truth is, it doesn't feel like loss anymore. Not entirely. I don't get sad in the same way I used to. There are still sharp moments—songs I skip, movies I avoid, the ache of wishing you were beside me when I have good news to share—but there's also peace. Over time, I've realized that in the stillness of those moments, because you're there.

I can still hear your laugh, see your dazzling smile, and hear your voice when I need it most. You live in my choices, my habits, the way I care for things—people, my beloved dog, maybe even myself. You're woven into the man I've become.

My heart and head are firmly in the present, looking toward the future, but the life we built remains my foundation. It shaped me, steadied me, made me better. And even after all this time, I know this much is true: I haven't really lost you at all.

And I never will.

Always,
Ron

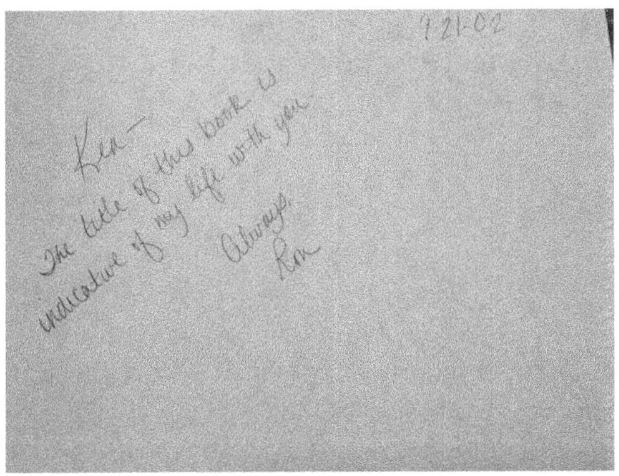

The inscription I wrote to him.

Author's Note:

This letter was my way of measuring distance—not in years, but in growth. For a long time, I thought healing meant getting over loss. It doesn't. It means learning to carry it differently—to make room for it, to let it become part of the landscape instead of the horizon.

When I wrote this, I realized I was no longer walking through grief—I was walking with it. It had become quieter, lighter, almost companionable. What I once called "loss" now feels more like inheritance: the humor, the creativity, the love we built—all of it still guiding me forward.

Ten years after losing Ken, I didn't find closure. I found continuation. And that's what love, at its purest, really is—something that refuses to end, even when everything else does.

VAMPIRES HAVE BEEN HERE

I woke up on October 1, 2011, with one hell of a hangover. Actually, it was a hangover plus.

The night before, I'd gone to see 50/50—the movie where Joseph Gordon-Levitt, who plays a young guy with cancer and Seth Rogen, who plays his friend. I figured Seth Rogen would make the topic palatable. What could go wrong? It had been only four months since Ken died, so in hindsight, it was a terrible idea. But I wanted to be okay—desperately, prematurely okay. It seemed like something Ken and I would have gone to see together, so I went alone.

At the historic Davis Theater in Lincoln Square, I felt awkward surrounded by couples. I couldn't remember the last time I saw a movie, but undoubtedly, it had been with Ken. But I texted my sister-in-law, Katie, who was my familiar cheerleader and posted on Facebook to prove I was "out in the world." Progress, right? The movie was actually good. I left feeling smugly triumphant, walking home under a pink sky, convinced I'd just had a breakthrough. Ken would've been proud.

Back home, I celebrated in my favorite way: with a frozen

Red Baron pizza, a few glasses of wine, and comfort TV—probably something nostalgic like The Bionic Woman or Charlie's Angels. Gems from a childhood that didn't know anything about grief or loss.

Then I popped an Ambien so I could get to bed early. Sleep had been elusive since Ken's death, so I'd gotten a prescription from my doctor for this miracle pill that was supposed to solve my problem. Except, it was the cause of most of them. Especially this one because I'd discovered its little secret: if you take it and stay awake, you drift into a euphoric, floaty space where feelings can't quite reach you. Harmless enough, I thought, for someone who had experienced more feelings than I appreciated in the last few years.

While I was getting ready for bed, my mother-in-law called. She wanted to know how the movie was because when we last spoke, I told her I'd be walking down the street to see it. We talked for a while—two people still on the inside of grief, trying to coach each other through. She told me she was joining a grief group, inspired by my doing the same. I was proud of her. I didn't tell her mine wasn't going well.

The next morning, I woke up groggy, my head pounding, stomach sloshing. I scrolled through my phone and froze at a text I'd sent the night before to my friend Mindy: "Vampires have been here."

Cue full-body cringe.

Flashes came back—I genuinely believed vampires had already been in my apartment and were returning to come back in again. My addled brain thought it made sense to text Mindy. To warn her. To let her know I was fighting a supernatural battle I might not win. She'd kindly humored me. Everyone handled me gently at the time, knowing I was fragile.

But the embarrassment wasn't the worst part. The worst

part was realizing how far from okay I really was—and that someone else might know it. In my mind, I still represented Ken. If I fell apart, it reflected poorly on him. Desperate for normalcy, I dragged myself out of bed, downed coffee, and walked to Paper Source to buy Christmas cards. Ken and I had always made our own, but I couldn't face that. Still, I wanted something familiar.

Halfway home on the walk, Mindy had called and texted me several times, but I couldn't answer. I was falling into a dark hole of realization that I wasn't exceptional in my grief.

"You sounded fine when we talked." Her most recent text message read.

We talked?! I had no memory of that. But sure enough, there it was in my call log—a 40-minute phone call. Plus an email with a home-protection spell I'd apparently performed to keep the vampires out. It involved herbs. And intention. Somewhere between Ambien and Cabernet, I'd become a witch. (No hate for the witches out there because I performed like I needed it!)

That night, what I thought was progress turned out to be another kind of reckoning—a reminder that healing can't be fast-forwarded. I wanted to be fine. Grief wanted me to be honest.

When Mindy visited later, she teased, "I thought maybe you were just in tune with otherworldly stuff."

"You thought it was normal that I believed vampires had been in my house?" I said, laughing so hard I fell back on the couch.

"Maybe you were a sensitive! Your metaphysical defenses were low." She was working overtime to gift me as much slack as possible.

"Oh, they were low all right," I said. "Low to the mixture of drugs and alcohol. I checked the photos on my phone. Turns out I even went out for a drink that night, too."

She gasped. "Where?"

"The bar where Ken and I met." I didn't remember much—just flashes. "Pretty sure I only had one drink and went home."

"Pretty sure?"

"Luckily, I'll never know what I said or who I saw." Take that, grief. I took the Ambien that caused so much supernaturally fueled chaos and used it to my advantage.

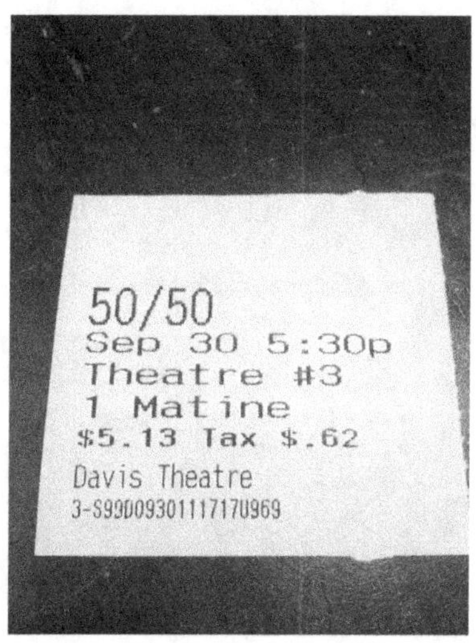

The ticket stub from the movie that knocked me
for a loop.

Author's Note:

In the early months after Ken died, I mistook movement for healing. If I could just go out, check a few boxes, act normal—I'd be fine. But grief doesn't reward performance. It waits until you're honest.

That night taught me something I couldn't have learned any other way: pretending to be okay is exhausting, but being human—even in all its messy, wine-soaked, Ambien-fueled chaos—is its own kind of grace.

Grief doesn't only break you open; sometimes, it breaks you

loose. And if you're lucky, you can laugh at the wreckage later, surrounded by people who love you enough to hold your absurdities with tenderness.

BAKING LESSONS

Yesterday I decided to bake an apple pie. Simple enough, right? But since I'd never made one before, it felt like a worthy challenge—no matter how it turned out. Worst case, I'd pitch it and learn something. (Call it "what if?" therapy-in-action.)

At Jewel, I couldn't find the pre-made pie dough. "Fine," I thought. "I'll make it myself." Google confirmed I had all the ingredients and warned the dough needed to chill for four hours or overnight. Perfect. Dough tonight, pie tomorrow. Easy peasy.

The next afternoon, post-therapy, I rolled out the buttery dough and nestled it into the pie dish for a pre-bake. No one likes a soggy bottom. Cooking shows had taught me that dried beans work as pie weights. A dusty bag of lentils in the cabinet—finally, a purpose! I poured them in, feeling smugly resourceful.

While the crust baked, my phone rang. It was Dave from the property management company—Awesome Dave, who'd helped make our apartment handicap-friendly after Ken's surgery.

"So, what are we gonna do?" he asked after a long preamble. "About...?"

"The rent."

"I'm confused. I paid the rent." I remember very clearly dropping it off early the morning Ken died—something to do to get me out of the house.

"No, you didn't," he accused.

"Yes, I did." I'd pulled up the bank website and logged in as soon as he mentioned the rent. It cleared on the third—a week ago.

"I'll call you back." Click.

I stewed while waiting for him to call back. He had the nerve to call me and accuse me of not paying my rent without simply checking first. I was furious when he called back because the home I shared with Ken was being called into question. I had no intention of leaving.

"The landlord wants to know if you're staying—if you can afford it," he said when he called back.

"Yes," I said flatly. "I'm staying." Then I hung up.

I know he wasn't trying to be cruel. But it stung. Maybe he didn't know the story. Maybe he did. Either way, it was another reminder that the world had already moved on while I was still standing still. When the call ended, I muttered, "What a dick."

The timer beeped. I pulled out the crust and poured off the lentils—well, most of them. The bottom layer had baked into the crust like decorative tile. Perfect. I stared at it, furious. I was trying to do something new, something fun, and now this? I wanted to toss the whole thing in the trash.

Instead, I sat down to journal. Halfway through, the truth landed. Ken would have fixed this. He could fix anything—the fixiest fixer ever. He'd have wrapped me in his arms, told me to calm down, maybe shaken me a martini. The problem wasn't the pie. It was the absence.

I closed my journal, curled up with *9 to 5* (a movie Ken and

I loved to watch while he was in hospice), and cried until I fell asleep.

When I woke, something had shifted. I peeked into the kitchen. The crust waited, smug. On a whim, I poked a lentil—and it popped out. Then another. And another. Soon the crust was clean again, ready for the apples I'd prepped the day before. Before I knew it, I was sealing the top crust and sliding it into the oven.

All was not lost.

For a first attempt, I'd give myself a "B." But the real lesson wasn't about baking—it was about patience, persistence, and letting grief cool before serving.

'Scuse me while I kiss this pie.

My first apple pie on a memorable day.

Author's Note:

When I wrote this, I realized that so much of early grief was just me trying to do something right again. To make order out of chaos. To prove I could still follow a recipe and get something beautiful out of the mess.

But this essay isn't really about pie. It's about the quiet art of starting over when nothing feels fixable. About learning that burned edges don't mean failure—they mean you're trying, you're present, you're alive.

Grief, like baking, takes patience. You follow the steps, make mistakes, scrape out what you can, and begin again. And sometimes—when you least expect it—what rises out of the wreckage is something warm, imperfect, and completely yours.

WIDOWER NO MORE

There was a time I never thought I'd be doing what I was doing. But there I was—standing in the middle of my living room on a bright, indifferent Saturday morning—packing up the last photos of Ken and me. The sun angled through the blinds in thin, decisive stripes, landing across the coffee table like a spotlight on the stack of frames I'd been avoiding for months. Maybe years.

The air in the room felt different that day. A little stiller. A little quieter. My Chow Chow Kallie's toenails clicked across the hardwood as she paced around me before settling in a heap on the rug in front of the fireplace, as if even she understood this was one of those turning-point moments. The kind you don't announce, but you feel in your bones.

I picked up the first frame—an old photo booth strip from Navy Pier. Ken's eyebrows were raised in that way that dared me not to laugh. I traced the edge of the frame with my thumb, then wrapped it in tissue paper. There was no lump in my throat, no sting behind my eyes. Just a calm, steady certainty. A feeling that surprised me with its clarity.

I slid the wrapped photo into the box and reached for the

next. By the third or fourth, I realized something almost startling: I didn't feel devastated. I didn't even feel resigned. I felt... ready.

Five and a half years had passed. That's long enough for a houseplant to become a tree or for a child to learn long division, but in grief time, it's barely a breath. Still, somewhere along the way, those photos—once sacred lifelines I clung to like oxygen—had become emotional drag. They pulled me backward just enough to keep my feet from moving forward. I needed to stop being Ron, the widower and start being Ron, period.

I'd told myself I'd already arrived there. I'd believed it, too. But grief has a mind of its own. It doesn't unfold in neat chapters or polite progressions. It loops and spirals, circles back when you least expect it, taps you on the shoulder in the middle of a grocery store, or hits you like a rogue wave while you're unloading the dishwasher. So I met this new phase with both gratitude and suspicion. Maybe this was another false floor that would give way beneath me (it's happened before). Grief can be generous like that—letting you think you've advanced to the next level before dropping you back where you started, bewildered and breathless.

By the time 2016 rolled in, it brought its own cruel math: fifteen years since we met, five since he died. I stood in the kitchen one night doing a lazy mental calculation and realized he'd now been gone for half the time we were together. Someday, he'd be gone longer than we ever were—and that still knocks the wind out of me, like someone quietly opening a trapdoor in the middle of the day.

But life had filled in around the loss. I'd built a home two blocks from the apartment where he'd drawn his last breath. Some people might avoid that proximity, but for me, it felt like a gentle nod to continuity. A way of honoring the life we built without freezing myself inside it.

I had good friends. I had meaningful work. I had actual laughter again—laughs that didn't feel borrowed or forced or apologetic. That part took the longest. Joy, when it finally returned, felt like an unexpected houseguest ringing the doorbell at dusk. You want to welcome it, but you open the door slowly, just in case.

The famous stages of grief never lined up for me the way the textbooks suggest. I skipped denial and bargaining completely, like someone flipping past a chapter that didn't apply to their life. I saved my anger for after he was gone, when the incomprehensibility finally caught up with me. Sadness and rage took turns leading the dance for years, long after I thought I'd made peace, long after everyone else assumed I had.

Even when I started dating again in 2013—something that felt both rebellious and necessary—I still needed people to know about Ken. That he existed. That our love was real. That my story didn't begin with them. I wasn't asking for permission or reassurance. I was validating my own life. Saying, 'here is where I come from. Here is who shaped me. Here is the truth of my heart.'

But somewhere along the line—quietly, without ritual or fanfare—I realized part of me was still waiting for him to come back. Not literally. Emotionally. Spiritually. Metaphorically. As if the story hadn't updated in my heart, like a software program that never installed the latest version. That realization landed with a thud and a flutter at the same time. He's not coming back. And I can still move forward. Somehow, that truth was both devastating and liberating.

The truth is, the longer I live, the smaller a portion of my life he occupies. Not in meaning—because that part is permanent—but in proportion. Loss fades as life expands. Love doesn't dim; it just moves over a little to make space for everything else.

That shift doesn't erase him. It honors him. It means I'm still living. Still discovering. Still here.

I used to speak in we and our. Our friends. Our apartment. Our plans. It was my default setting. Now it's I, me, and my. It still tastes unfamiliar sometimes, like switching from your usual brand of coffee to something bolder and darker. But it also tastes right. Ken's story is woven into mine forever—stitched into the seams—but I no longer need to lead with loss. I no longer need to present myself as the after version of someone else's ending.

Eventually, I got to the last photo. The two of us standing on the lakefront in coats too thin for the weather, laughing as the Chicago wind whipped our hair into chaos. I wrapped it gently and placed it on top of the others. The box was full now, soft with tissue and heavy with history.

I closed the flaps and reached for a thick black marker. I didn't think too hard about it; I just wrote the first word that came to mind: RELICS. Not artifacts. Not memories. Relics. Pieces of something sacred, something from another life.

I didn't cry. I didn't hesitate. I sealed the box and stood back, palms flat on the cardboard for a quiet beat. The room felt lighter. My chest felt looser. Even the air seemed to open up a little.

Someday—maybe years from now—I'll unpack that box and let those memories mingle freely with the present. I'll spread the photos out on the floor, pour a drink, and sit with them as easily as I sit with my own reflection. But not yet. Not today.

Today, I'm content knowing I've crossed a quiet threshold. A line I couldn't name until I stepped over it.

I'm a widower no more.

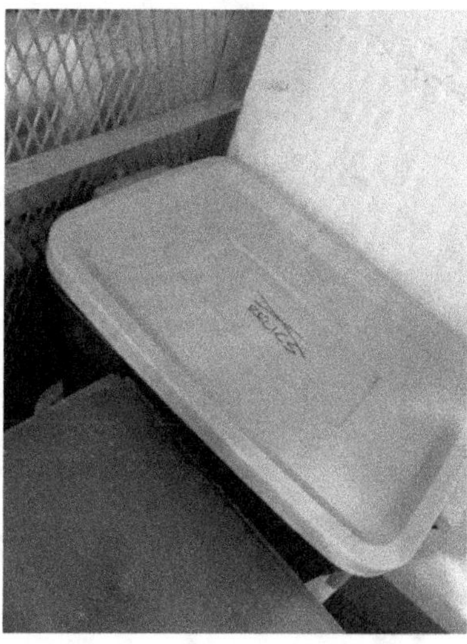

Though I eventually reincorporated these "relics"
back into my life, this felt like an important step.

Author's Note:

This piece marks a line I didn't know I was allowed to cross until I found myself standing on the other side of it. For a long time, being a widower felt less like a descriptor and more like an identity I was required to carry, almost as proof of love. Letting go of that label felt risky. As if naming myself differently might suggest I was leaving Ken behind, or minimizing what we had.

Writing this essay helped me see that wasn't true.

Packing up those photos wasn't about erasing him or moving on in the tidy way people like to imagine grief works. It was about acknowledging that my life had grown larger than the loss that once defined it. That shift didn't happen all at once, and it didn't come with fireworks or closure. It arrived quietly, disguised as readiness.

I include this reflection here because so many people navigating loss feel pressure to either stay frozen in it or prove they've "overcome" it. I don't believe in either extreme. Grief changes shape over time. It loosens its grip. It moves from the center to the margins, where it can still be honored without running the show.

If this essay resonates, I hope it offers reassurance that crossing a threshold doesn't mean forgetting where you came from. It means trusting that the love you've known is sturdy enough to remain part of you, even when it's no longer the headline.

There is life after loss. Not instead of it. Alongside it. And sometimes, naming that truth is its own quiet act of courage.

IN THE GROOVE

In 2018, I decided that turning fifty deserved something bigger than dinner reservations and a well-lit selfie. So, I flew to Costa Rica with my college bestie, Denise—a long-held friend who had witnessed more versions of myself than anyone else.

We landed in the capital, already sweating before our luggage even appeared on the carousel, and spent the next few days chasing waterfalls, dodging lizards with an unsettling amount of confidence, and eating plantains in every possible form. It was the kind of trip you take when you're old enough to know how rare moments like this are, but still young enough to get sunburned because you forgot the sunscreen in the room.

One morning, we visited a small cacao farm tucked into the hills. The air was thick in that way tropical air always seems to be—like someone draped a warm, damp blanket over the entire country. The guide led us down a narrow path between trees heavy with fruit and cracked open a cacao pod. Inside were beans coated in a white, slimy pulp that looked nothing like the chocolate bars that have always doubled as my emotional support system. If you've never tasted raw cacao, let me tell you: it is bitter enough to make your soul pucker. But the bitterness wasn't the thing that stayed with me.

The farmer, a man whose hands told the story—someone who worked with the land, not with spreadsheets, stepped into the shade and showed us how grafting works. I'd heard the word before, but never seen it up close. It's surprisingly tender. He took one young plant—soft, green, vulnerable—and made a careful slit in its stem. Then he took a piece of another plant, freshly cut and pulsing with its own life, and slid it into the opening. He wrapped the two together with tape, snug and intentional.

"This one has the strength," he said, pointing to the donor plant. "This one has the flavor." He tapped the graft. "Together, they survive better."

I remember standing there, sweating through my shirt, with Denise beside me snapping photos and asking questions like the journalist she'll always be at heart. I only managed one photo, but I didn't ask anything. I just watched. Because something in that moment went straight to a place inside me I didn't know was waiting to be touched.

Life splits us open. Sometimes gently. Sometimes, like a storm blowing a door off its hinges. What gets added afterward —who gets added—can change how we grow from that point forward.

Ken was grafted into me. That was certain—obvious. I'd walked through my own storm years earlier when Ken died. That loss had cut me open in ways no one could prepare you for, not even the hospice nurse who gently tells you to eat something, even though you can't imagine doing anything normal ever again. In the years after his death, I kept trying to grow from the place I'd been split, not realizing that growth wasn't about sealing myself back up. It was about what I allowed to be grafted in. New people. New rituals. New ways of understanding myself in a world that didn't look the same.

Sitting there in Costa Rica, watching a farmer bind two separate pieces into one stronger whole, something clicked. It wasn't a lightning bolt. More like the quiet realization that I, too, was made of many parts—some I chose, some I didn't, some that were handed to me when the life I knew fell apart.

The tape that held those new pieces together didn't look like anything impressive. It looked like journaling late at night when my heart felt too big for my chest. It looked like friends who sat with me in silence because they didn't know what to say, and that was okay. It looked like getting a dog again, years later, and remembering that joy doesn't erase loss, but it can sit beside it without apology. It looked like letting myself build a new life without pretending the old one didn't matter.

That day on the farm, I realized that grafting isn't about replacing what was. It's about strengthening what remains. It's about acknowledging that we become sturdier not by resisting the breaks, but by accepting what grows in the space they leave behind. I carried that idea home with me. Not consciously at first. It lived quietly in the background, the way most truths do, until I caught myself recognizing the ways I'd been grafted without even knowing it.

The older I get, the more I understand that growth isn't a solo act. We're always being shaped by who and what gets added to our lives. Sometimes we choose it. Sometimes fate does. Sometimes it's a beautiful choice. Sometimes it's bitter like raw cacao. But bitterness can be part of the recipe too. It doesn't make the final product any less worth savoring.

When I think about that farm now, I remember the heat, the sweetness of the air, the sound of leaves brushing against each other in the breeze. But mostly, I remember the quiet truth wrapped in that simple demonstration. Strength doesn't come from standing alone. It comes from being willing to become something new.

And at fifty, in the middle of a Costa Rican hillside surrounded by cacao, coffee, and one very patient farmer, I finally understood that becoming stronger often starts with being split open—and trusting what gets grafted in next.

Grafted coffee plant—the only picture I took on
the tour.

Author's Note:

This essay started as a travel memory, the kind you tuck away because it felt meaningful, but you're not quite sure why yet. It wasn't until much later, rereading my own words, that I realized how often I've returned to that image of grafting when I try to make stense of my life after loss.

Grief has a way of convincing us that strength means sealing ourselves off, learning to stand alone, proving we can survive without what we lost. What this moment in Costa Rica taught me, slowly and gently, is that survival often looks more like integration than isolation. The things and people that came into my life after Ken's death didn't replace him. They didn't erase what we had. They joined me in the places where I'd been split open.

This essay lives here because it marks one of those quiet internal shifts. Not a breakthrough you announce to anyone, just a truth you begin carrying differently. If you're reading this while navigating your own fractures, I hope it offers permission to let new strength in without guilt. To believe that what grows next can honor what came before.

We are not meant to be whole all by ourselves. And becoming something new doesn't mean losing what mattered. Sometimes it's exactly how we keep it.

PART III: THE GROUND BENEATH ME

WHEN THE DUST SETTLES, YOU FIND THE SOIL WAS CHANGING ALL ALONG

THE LUCK WE CARRY

Every so often, you meet someone who changes the temperature of your day—not through grand gestures or deep conversations, but through a single, simple truth. That happened to me recently at the library book sale where I volunteer. I didn't know her name, and she'll probably never know how much her words stayed with me. But sometimes, that's the beauty of small encounters—they arrive quietly and leave something behind.

"I don't understand why some people are so lucky," she said sweetly, without a hint of complaint. It wasn't self-pity—just a quiet truth she'd been carrying for a long time. "I've had three heart attacks, diabetes, and cancer. And some people go through life with no problems."

She was tiny and frail, the kind of small that makes you instinctively want to protect her. Wisps of gray hair escaped what might have once been a careful bun, fluttering in the cool October breeze. Her cardigan hung loosely from narrow shoulders, and the sleeves brushed her hands as she moved. There was a faint floral scent about her—like talcum powder and old perfume—and her steps were slow but deliberate, each one placed carefully as if the ground itself might shift beneath her.

When she spoke, her voice trembled just slightly, but not from weakness—more like someone who's learned that words should be handled gently. Her blue eyes were bright and steady, carrying that rare combination of fragility and strength that makes you stop and pay attention.

I offered to carry the books she'd just bought at the library book sale—one of my favorite weekends of the year. The place hums with energy: paper bags rustling, pages flipping, volunteers calling out prices over the low murmur of conversation. The air smelled like paper, dust, and a hint of coffee from the staff room down the hall. It's a lot of work, but it's deeply satisfying—a joyful kind of chaos for people who understand the quiet magic of books.

As we walked to her car, I found myself moved by the simplicity of her statement. She wasn't complaining. She was just noticing. There was something almost pure about that—someone acknowledging the unevenness of life without bitterness or blame.

"I guess most people couldn't handle everything you've had to deal with," I said as I set the bags in her trunk.

Her bright blue eyes darted at me, then away. "Do you think so?" she asked softly, almost like she was tasting the idea.

"Well, you're still here, aren't you? I think that's proof."

She paused for a moment, as if weighing the truth in what I said. A soft smile began to form, the kind that comes from being seen, I hoped.

"Thank you for helping me with the books," she said, smiling before slipping into her car.

"See you at the Spring Sale!" I called after her, waving.

When she drove off, I stood there for a moment, the wind catching the loose strands of my hair, the faint scent of paper still clinging to my hands. I thought about how some people carry their luck quietly—not as something good or bad, but simply as life itself, unfolding one page at a time.

That night, I wrote about her in my journal. Not to analyze the moment, but to hold onto it—the reminder that perspective is a kind of grace. Sometimes, journaling isn't about finding answers. It's about noticing the people and moments that soften us, one story at a time.

An image I created to remind me of the irony of love and loss.

Author's Note:

This essay reminds me that grief doesn't always speak in thunderclaps. Sometimes, it shows up in whispers—in passing conversations, quiet realizations, and strangers who unknowingly hold a mirror to your heart.

The woman at the library didn't know my story, and I didn't know hers. But her words found me at a time when I was still learning how to live alongside loss, not under it. What struck me most was her tone—not self-pitying or defeated, just...accepting. She'd made peace with the unevenness of life, the way joy and pain coexist without canceling each other out.

For years, I'd thought of luck as something external—something you either have or don't. But that day shifted my definition. Luck isn't about being spared from hardship; it's about surviving it with your tenderness intact.

Every time I volunteer at the book sale now, I look for her—not expecting to see her, but to remember her lesson. That grace doesn't always arrive wrapped in grand meaning. Sometimes it comes in a paper bag full of used books and a reminder that we're all, in our own ways, carrying a bit of luck—just to still be here, still noticing.

AND THEN THE UNIVERSE WINKED

"Now that we have a quiet moment," Deb, the volunteer coordinator, said, pulling me aside during a lull at the library book sale.

Her tone was unusually serious. My first thought: Uh oh. She's going to tell me to tone it down. I'd been my usual self—chatty, laughing, maybe a little louder than your average bibliophile.

What she said next caught me off guard. It probably caught others off guard, too, when I moved from Chicago to the north-west suburbs during the pandemic. If I'm being honest, it surprised me a little as well. But at the time, it made complete sense. Only later did I understand why it didn't to everyone else —it was an unexpected plot twist in a story that, from the outside, looked firmly rooted in the city.

For years, I'd loved Chicago. The energy, the noise, the heartbeat of it all—it felt like being part of something alive. I loved the L rattling by, the smell of rain on hot pavement, the hum of people moving through their days.

Until I didn't.

When the world shrank, so did my love for the chaos. My

life didn't change much logistically—I'd worked from home for years—but something inside me shifted. The city started to feel tight, like a suit that no longer fit. The crowds that once comforted me began to suffocate. I wanted space. Light. Silence.

When mortgage rates dropped, and luck was on my side, I bought my first house. No shared walls. A yard. Birds instead of sirens (though the fire station around the corner likes to remind me the suburbs have a similar soundtrack). The quiet was startling at first, then soothing. It was mine.

But quiet can only take you so far. Eventually, I needed connection again. I've always been someone who builds community wherever I land—at work, at the dog park, in line at the coffee shop. It was a trait I already possessed, but one that sharpened in my life with Ken, and even more so after he died. Every year I had him seemed to unlock new levels inside me. So, when I saw a flyer for the library's used book sale, I went. I left with two cookbooks and a feeling I hadn't expected: this is where I belong.

A few months later, I joined the Friends of the Library and started volunteering at the sales. They became one of my favorite things—lively, low-stakes, full of kind, quirky people who love stories as much as I do.

"Would you consider joining the board?" Deb asked, her kind eyes smiling. "You have a lot to offer."

My brain thought, "but you'd need an adult for that," though I managed a smile instead. I was stunned—and deeply touched. I don't remember much of what she said after that because I was busy absorbing something I hadn't realized I'd been missing. I'd been seen. Not for who I was trying to be, but for who I already was.

It was such a small, ordinary moment—but it felt quietly monumental—like finding buried treasure in my own backyard. And I greedily and giddily accepted the offer.

Even now, I sometimes measure my life against the one I might have had if Ken were still here. Not in sadness, just awareness. When he was alive, I played the blissful introvert, happily orbiting his extroverted energy. Now, I play both parts —cherishing solitude while also reaching toward connection. That's my new story. The plot twist.

All these years later, I'm still finding my way back to belonging—sometimes in a crowded city, sometimes in a quiet suburban library surrounded by used books and good people.

Either way, it feels like home.

One of my favorite things to do is volunteer at our library book sales. Ken would love it for me, too.

Author's Note:

When I left Chicago, I thought I was stepping away from something—the noise, the pace, the version of myself that belonged to another chapter. What I didn't realize was that I was also stepping toward something: a quieter kind of purpose, the kind that doesn't announce itself with fanfare but with an unexpected invitation in the middle of a book sale.

For years after Ken died, I searched for meaning in big ways —through writing, travel, reinvention. But lately, I've learned that belonging can be built from smaller gestures: showing up, stacking books, making people laugh in between checkout lines.

This piece isn't really about moving to the suburbs or joining a library board. It's about the way life keeps handing us new scenes to play—even when we think the show is over.

The greatest comfort of this season has been realizing that connection doesn't need to be loud to be profound. Sometimes it begins quietly, with a stranger pulling you aside to say, "You have something to offer."

And sometimes, that's all the reminder you need that you still do.

FOR THE LOVE OF HER

I flew to Los Angeles for my sister-in-law Katie's memorial. Even seeing that sentence on the screen still doesn't compute. Her death had come as a shock, especially considering we were the same age. It was a trip I both dreaded and needed—wanting to be with family, unwilling to accept why.

My brother-in-law, Craig, asked me to speak—to tell a story about Katie. I was honored, humbled, and a little terrified. Craig and my nephews—the boys, now grown into kind, remarkable men—spoke before me. Their words were beautiful: funny, fierce, and full of love. Katie would have been so proud. I know I was.

The church overflowed. Extra chairs appeared as more people arrived, which surprised no one. Katie was a giver, a connector, a collector of people. She built community like it was muscle memory—gathering friends like seashells, each one unique, each one cherished. Everyone wanted to be there, to share a story, to stand in the glow of her light one more time.

When my turn came, I felt myself leave my body. I remember speaking but not being in it—as if a thin wall stood between my heart and my voice, just sturdy enough to keep me from falling apart. Others spoke too—close friends Laurie, Gayle, and so many others who'd known different versions of her. Like a finely cut diamond, Katie had a hundred facets, each catching light in its own way.

The story I told was from her visit to Chicago, when Ken was in home hospice. She surprised him with a tattoo—a tiny PadLo, the stuffed animal their friend Renee had made, and Ken adored. When she showed it to him, he grinned and said, "I want one."

Of course, Katie made it happen. She called it their "A Grand Day Out." She bundled him into his wheelchair, took him throughout the city, and somehow convinced an in-demand tattoo artist to fit him in. It was their last great adventure together—pure joy and mischief and love. So very Katie.

After the service, people lingered in clusters, talking quietly. I kept catching myself looking for her—glancing at Craig, then at the boys, then at Mama Jo—and scanning the crowd for someone I knew I wouldn't find. And yet, she was everywhere.

That's the strange mercy of loss: it doesn't take everything. The body leaves, but the energy remains. Her laugh. Her warmth. The way she made everyone feel seen. They live on in the people who loved her, stitched into our days like bright thread.

Katie was a librarian—passionate about stories and helping others find theirs. At the service, we each wrote a memory and slipped it into books stacked near the podium. When it was my turn, I was handed *Remarkably Bright Creatures* by Shelby Van Pelt. No one there could have known it was the very book I'd just finished back home, borrowed from my local library.

It felt like her—subtle, clever, perfectly timed. A wink from beyond the stacks. Her presence lingers in every story she inspired, every laugh she sparked, every life she touched. And maybe that's the truest kind of legacy—love that never really leaves the room.

My sister-in-law Katie and Ken had a very special and sweet relationship.

Author's Note:

Grief has a strange way of reminding us that love isn't linear. When Ken died, I thought I understood loss—the before, the after, the permanent shift between the two. But when Katie died, I realized how grief expands to make room for every person we've ever loved. Each loss feels new, yet somehow connects to all the ones that came before it.

Katie's death reopened something tender in me—not a wound, but a doorway. Standing at her memorial, surrounded by family, I could feel Ken there too. It wasn't painful the way it once would have been. It was comforting, like two threads of the same story weaving together.

She and I shared more than family. We shared Ken. His memory was our meeting place—our shorthand, our humor, our proof that love outlasts the people who start it.

Writing this piece reminded me how legacy works. It's not

the big, dramatic moments that define us. It's the small acts of care—the tattoo, the book, the shared laughter that keep echoing years later. Katie taught me that you don't have to stay to keep giving. Some people's light simply lingers. Hers does. Ken's does.

And maybe that's what all of us who grieve come to learn in time: the people we love don't leave; they just change form. They live on in every story we tell about them, every kindness we offer because they once offered it to us.

WE STILL ARE

I didn't expect to make a new friend while Ken was in home hospice. My hands were full; my heart was bruised. But friendship sometimes finds you when you're too tired to perform and too broken to pretend.

Claire was Ken's hospice grief counselor. She started visiting weekly since that dizzying week he came home from his final hospital stay. I was juggling logistics—equipment, medication, visitors, my own unraveling—and she arrived quietly, intuitively, with a silky voice that seemed designed to calm a house in chaos.

"Hi, I'm Claire," she said, smiling.

"Hi, Claire. I'm Ron."

I led her through the back door so Ken could rest undisturbed in the front room. My father-in-law had the coffee table flipped over to fix a leg—"Glad I'm not the only thing in here with a bad leg," Ken, an amputee, liked to joke. His brother and our nephew were unpacking groceries. The place was full of movement, noise, and love.

I gave Claire time alone with Ken. I knew her visits would help him—and, though I didn't realize it yet, me, too.

Before long, I started looking forward to her knock. My world had shrunk to caregiving and survival, one moment at a time. When Claire arrived, my shoulders relaxed. Ken adored her. Their laughter—loud and contagious—spilled down the hallway, reminding me there was still life in the house.

She spoke his language: creation, wonder, delight. He'd ask me to pull out his art so he could show her. Preparing for her visits began to feel like preparing for company. We joked that, in another timeline, we'd have been friends anyway—Chicago or LA, hospice or not. Some connections feel inevitable. The lesson landed deep: even in the darkest seasons, stay open. The universe still delivers gifts.

Claire came every week until May 26, 2011—her last visit before moving back to LA. She said goodbye to me and, impossibly, to him. He understood she was leaving and was happy for her. He was also saying a final goodbye to someone he loved.

After Ken died, Claire and I texted occasionally. In August, she wrote that she'd be in Chicago for a quick trip and that we should get together for a drink. We planned to meet at Tiny Lounge in my neighborhood. I hadn't seen her since that day in May when she came to say goodbye. Grief still sat just below the surface; I wondered if I'd fall apart the moment I saw her.

I saw her as soon as I turned the corner. She was at a sidewalk table, long brown hair swept to one side. She smiled, and we hugged tightly. It felt lighter this time—like stepping into sunlight after a long winter.

"How are you?" she asked.

"I'm fine," I said automatically—then realized I meant it. She smiled softly.

"Let me ask a better question," she said, this not being her first grief rodeo. "How do you think you're doing?"

I laughed. "Some days are better. Some days not. One step forward, two back."

She nodded. "Ken was a big presence. I think of him often."

"I don't even know if it's 'thinking' about him," I said. "He's part of me. So he's in everything."

"That makes sense," she said. "How is it being alone in the apartment?"

"Honestly? Good. I rearranged some rooms—because I can."

She smiled. "I remember that feeling after my dad died—sad and strange, but also this quiet joy in putting something somewhere and having it stay."

"Ken was the orderly one," I said. "Now nothing's out of place. It's...spartan. I like it."

"I do too." She paused. "I've been thinking about the last time I saw him."

"That was a rough day," I said.

She nodded. "Did he tell you what we talked about?"

"No. I wanted him to have his own space."

"You two had such a strong connection," she said. "It was obvious."

I paused, a smile spreading across my face. Despite the limited time we had together, our relationship remains one of the things I'm most proud of. It was equal. Even. Supportive. Loving. Creative. Everything I'd ever hoped for. It was easy to lose myself in the thought of it.

Her eyes held steady. "I asked Ken if there was anything he wanted me to tell you after he was gone."

The world grew quiet around me except for the growing sound of my heartbeat as I considered that Ken and Claire shared words that I wasn't aware of. A conspiracy hidden from me for months.

"He loved you so much, Ron. I typed his words into my phone as he spoke, so I'd have it exact. I still have it. I...I just wanted to see you first before I sent it. To make sure...to see how you were doing."

Even from the grave, Ken was taking care of my emotions as he had done dutifully during our life together. "Did I pass the test?" I asked, grinning.

"With flying colors," said, smiling. We toasted and finished our drinks.

We hugged goodbye under the glow of Lincoln Avenue streetlights. I told her I loved her. Then I walked home fast, adrenaline humming under my skin. Halfway there, I slowed, letting the August air press against me. I wanted to savor the anticipation of something extraordinary.

At home, I poured a glass of cabernet and sat in the garden Ken had so lovingly tended. The angel trumpets perfumed the air. I opened the email on my phone, chin trembling. And then I read aloud what my love had asked Claire to share with me:

I still am.
Together we still be.
We're still here.
We still exist together.

My heart surged and broke all over again. I read the words aloud, again and again, until they sounded like prayer. Gratitude rose behind the tears—gratitude for his clarity, his love, and for the messenger who waited until I was ready to receive them.

Those words became my compass. They named what I already knew: that connection doesn't end, it transforms. That love isn't erased by loss; it expands to hold what's gone.

I framed his message. It moves around the house, sometimes near our favorite photo from a movie night at Hollywood Forever Cemetery. His words follow me, steadying me, reminding me of who we were—who we still are.

Because every single word is true.

I keep the words close to a photo of us.

Author's Note:

Some stories live in the quiet space between worlds. This is one of them.

When Claire sent me Ken's message, it felt like time folded —as if past and present touched for a moment and exchanged breath. I'd spent months trying to learn how to live without him, and here was proof that I didn't have to. Not entirely.

For so long, I thought grief's job was to erase, to thin the connection until it disappeared. But this moment taught me the opposite: love isn't linear, and it doesn't obey death. It adapts. It finds new ways to exist—in memory, in language, in the stillness of a garden, in the echo of a shared laugh you can still hear if you listen closely enough.

Ken's message didn't resurrect him; it reframed him. It was the final gift in a long line of them—a reminder that I wasn't left behind, I was left with. With the lessons, the humor, the presence, the "we."

I think that's why I keep his words where I can see them. Not as proof of what was lost, but as evidence of what remains.

Love doesn't end. It evolves. And when we listen closely enough, it still speaks.

A MAN OF TWO WORLDS

I am a man of two worlds.

Trying to reconcile what I've built with what I've lost—how I can feel whole and broken in the same breath. How I can invest in the future while still longing for the past.

I'm inspired by the greatest love I've ever known and haunted by the greatest loss I've ever endured.

Each day feels like both sanctuary and prison—safe from pain, confined by absence. I often wonder if anyone has ever felt this exact way.

The love I carry fuels my creativity. The loss fractures who I'm still becoming.

I don't want to wear grief as a badge, but resisting it feels futile. Some days, I think it's all I am—or why I am.

Grief was once a shadow on the periphery—until it stepped

forward the day the doctor said the words. Since then, it's been both my witness and my companion.

I am a man of two worlds, driven to create—shaped by loss, still hopeful.

I can't celebrate my joys without honoring my sorrows; they're intertwined, like love and grief—inseparable, ordinary, divine.

Life doesn't end neatly, nor should it. It's the sum of all our contradictions—the triumphs and the tender wreckage we carry forward.

Half my breath belongs to the living; the other half resides in memory.

Grief is the quiet canopy above me—reminding me that gratitude and ache can coexist. The joy of my present will always hum with the ache of my past.

All these mismatched pieces make me whole. They don't fit perfectly, but they are mine.

Time folds in on itself, pressing new memories over old ones, reshaping what remains.

I am a man of two worlds.
Forever. Gladly. Forlornly.

From the day we got married in Iowa in 2009.

Author's Note:

This piece sits at the crossroads of who I was and who I've become. It's not about choosing between love and loss, but learning to live inside both at once.

In the early years after Ken's death, I thought grief was something to outgrow—a mountain to climb and descend. But over time, I realized it doesn't end. It integrates. It settles into the architecture of who you are, not as a scar, but as a supporting beam.

Writing this poem helped me name that duality. My joy and my sorrow aren't opposites—they coexist, braided together through memory and meaning. Every success carries his echo. Every quiet moment carries his absence.

But that's not tragedy—it's continuity. The love that once grounded me now moves through me, shaping how I create, connect, and see the world.

I am, and always will be, a man of two worlds. And I've learned that's not something to fix. It's something to honor.

PART IV: THE ORIGIN STORY

BEFORE LOVE AND LOSS, THERE WAS LAUGHTER—AND A BOY WHO LEARNED TO TELL STORIES

BULLY FOR ME

I tore through the town park, all adrenaline and fear. My small-town life had suddenly turned into a race for survival. He lunged and caught the sleeve of the class jacket I'd begged my parents to overpay for so I could feel like I belonged—or at least less like I didn't. But at nearly six feet tall and barely a hundred pounds, I was all legs. He slipped, hit the dirt, and went down hard.

I'd escaped. He hadn't taken anything from me. Or had he?

For the most part, my childhood was "normal." School came easily, but people didn't. I preferred television's tidy worlds to the chaos of the real one. Team sports terrified me. I was shy, skinny, soft-spoken—different in all the ways that drew attention for the wrong reasons.

By junior high, my difference made me a target. When isolation didn't protect me, humor became my armor. If I could make the bullies laugh—usually by making myself the punchline—I could survive the encounter. It was a strange kind of diplomacy, but it worked. Laughter, I learned, could be both shield and sword.

High school brought relief. I joined the newspaper, and by junior year, I was editor-in-chief. Writing gave me a voice. For the first time, people liked being around me—especially girls, which makes sense since they were experiencing puberty in the "normal" way, while I was struggling to understand who I was.

The hormones that should have been raging in me were apparently on sabbatical. So when I heard there was a girl who "liked" me, I was surprised—and unprepared. She was an eighth grader, which, even if I'd been interested, was laughably beneath a junior's social station. Still, part of me wondered if being liked might make me less of a target. Maybe it would buy me a little peace.

That fantasy lasted about three conversations. She giggled too much, said "cute" too often, and didn't know a thing about *Knots Landing*. My apartness won again. Unfortunately, she had her own admirer—a short, freckled, sharp-tongued nightmare named Howard. When he learned she liked me, he decided it was grounds for war. I laughed off rumors that he wanted to fight me. After all, he was in eighth grade. I was practically an adult.

Then, one spring afternoon, he started following me home. Sometimes he'd talk. Sometimes he'd politely ask if I wanted to fight. Sometimes he just trailed behind in silence. It was unsettling but mostly annoying. I just wanted to make it home in time for *General Hospital.* Luke and Laura were everything.

One day, he brought backup—a chubby henchman from my own class. They followed me through the pasture behind the school, hurling insults about how I walked, dressed, and looked. It was like a bad after-school special—minus the moral lesson and freeze-frame ending.

When I crossed into town, I thought I'd lost them. Then Howard shouted something cruel about "kicking my ass." I stopped by a tree, my heart hammering, unsure what to do. That's when the henchman charged—head down like a bull. I sidestepped, and he slammed straight into the tree. The sound was equal parts horrifying and hilarious.

I bolted. By the time I stopped running, I was alone. The fear faded, but the shame didn't. I hadn't done anything wrong, yet I felt humiliated. I walked the last few blocks home, blinking back tears. I couldn't show up crying. I was a junior. He was an eighth grader. It didn't add up.

My dad was in the garage, wearing goggles, cutting wood on the table saw. I waved and smiled, pretending I was fine, then hurried inside. Once the door shut, the tears came. Loud, shaking, unstoppable. The saw drowned out my sobs, and I was grateful for the noise.

I locked myself in the bathroom, gripping the sink. My reflection blurred behind tears. I yanked off my jacket and hurled it to the floor. The humiliation, confusion, and anger poured out of me like steam escaping a kettle. I could barely breathe.

I turned on the faucet to mask my crying and stared at my blotchy face in the mirror. Somewhere in that mess of sound and snot and saltwater, a thought rose up—quiet and clear.

"I like you," I whispered to my reflection.

I took a shaky breath. "I like you," I said again, louder this time. "I...like...you."

It was the first time I'd ever said it out loud—to anyone. In that moment, I didn't know much, but I knew this: I wouldn't be defined by someone else's cruelty. My misery was temporary. My difference was permanent. And one day, it would be my superpower.

That night, standing over the sink in a small Indiana bathroom, I met myself for the first time. And I really liked the guy.

I've walked through my hometown park many times, and I always think of tearing through it at breakneck speed on that pivotal day.

Author's Note:

This was the story I didn't know I'd been carrying all my life.

It's easy to think of bullying as something you "get over," but the truth is, those moments plant seeds—of fear, of resilience, of identity—that take years to grow into whatever they're meant to become. Writing this piece helped me trace the origin of a kind of quiet courage I didn't recognize at the time. That moment in front of the bathroom mirror was more than teenage defiance—it was self-recognition.

When I told my reflection, "I like you," I didn't yet know what that meant, not fully. I just knew it was the first honest thing I'd ever said to myself. It was the beginning of learning how to belong—to myself first, and then to the world.

This essay marks the shift from being shaped by other

people's opinions to shaping my own story. Looking back, I realize that kid who stood shaking in front of the mirror wasn't broken; he was becoming.

MOVIES AND RENTALS
AND BEARS, OH MY!

My ticket to Chicago was Blockbuster Video. In the 1990s, the iconic blue-and-yellow stores were as ubiquitous as Starbucks is today. It was just the opportunity I was looking forward to catapult myself from small-time Indiana to the big leagues of Chicago.

I'd always dreamed of living here, and after college—diploma in hand, no clue what I wanted to be when I grew up—I was working at a franchise in my college town in Indiana. Blockbuster was exploding everywhere at the time, so when I heard the owners talking about another franchisee in Chicago, I asked if they could ask about any openings. They did. And that's how I landed in Hoffman Estates in the summer of 1992, wearing a blue polo and rewinding tapes for a living.

The store was packed that summer—kids renting, kids working, a blur of VHS cases and teenage hormones. My crew was a sitcom cast: Dani the Princess, Brandy the Clown, Adam the Actor/Musician. Lazy but lovable, they were my first Chicago family. They'd swing by in tuxes and gowns before their school dances, then show up hungover for their shifts the next morning. They fought over who got to work with me on Christmas Day because I was a pushover and made it fun.

One afternoon, the staff started buzzing.

"That's Mike!"

"Mike's coming in!"

I had no idea who Mike was, but everyone else clearly did. He walked in—friendly but intense—and the staff practically lined up to greet him. When he came to my register to check out, I smiled. "Did you use to work here?"

He chuckled politely and left.

No wonder he didn't last, I thought. Kind of smug and rude to deal with the Northwest suburban clientele we served. "Kind of rude, huh?" I said to no one in particular. The entire staff burst into laughter. There was a joke I wasn't let in on.

"That's Mike Singletary," my manager said, barely able to control his laughter.

That meant nothing to me. "Is he a musician?" I blinked repeatedly.

Blank stare. "He's a Chicago Bear. Football."

"He still owes late fees," was all I could think to say.

It wasn't my last Bear encounter. Walter Payton's kids were regulars. Their account had a big, flashing note: DO NOT RENT WITHOUT A CARD. When they showed up empty-handed, I refused. They groaned; I stood firm.

Later that night, after sending them away without a rental, the phone rang. A high, clipped voice chewed me out for refusing to rent to the Payton kids. "I'm sorry, Mrs. Payton," I said. "But they need their card."

Click.

It wasn't Mrs. Payton. It was Walter himself. Apparently, he drove the kids back—with their card. Technically, I'd won.

Working retail is a rite of passage—like basic training, but with name tags and late fees. You learn how to deal with everyone: the kind, the cranky, the ones who think you personally control the supply of Beethoven 2.

The job was non-stop exhausting. But it was also the most fun I've ever had for the least amount of money. Back then, I dreamed of having weekends off, a salary, maybe even health insurance. Now I have all that—and still, part of me misses those Blockbuster nights: the hum of the fluorescent lights, the smell of plastic cases and popcorn, the easy laughter between customers and coworkers. It was the place to be on a weekend night, after all.

That job was more than a paycheck—it was a doorway. I'd moved to Chicago alone, a stranger to everything, with no idea who played for the Bears. Thirty years later, I still don't. But that summer, in that blue polo, I began building a life of my own —one rental at a time.

Please be kind. Rewind.

Ken howled when I told him this story. And I loved it.

Author's Note:

This story always makes me smile because it captures a

version of me who was still figuring out who he was—wide-eyed, uncertain, but already chasing something bigger.

At the time, I thought I was just trading VHS tapes for a paycheck. But really, I was learning how to connect—with people, with work, with a city that would eventually shape my adult life. That Blockbuster wasn't just my first Chicago address; it was my training ground in empathy, humor, and resilience.

What strikes me most looking back is how ordinary those nights were—and how extraordinary they became in memory. Sometimes the smallest, most unglamorous jobs become the foundation for the rest of your story. The lessons sneak in between rewinds.

THEY CALLED ME RONA

"So, tell me how you think the death of Kurt Cobain will impact music," a reporter asked me, ready to scribble my words of wisdom on a notepad.

I blinked. "Uh...let me get the manager."

I knew he'd died—it was tragic—but I didn't have a prepared statement for the media. I was only part-time.

A few years after college, I'd moved to Chicago with no grand plan beyond paying rent and collecting experiences. Like most twenty-somethings, I worked two jobs: one for the bills, one for "fun money." The fun one was at Coconuts, a now-defunct music store on the corner of Clark and Diversey.

It had everything I loved: music, people, and air-conditioning. I'd bought a few cassette singles there and loved the energy, so one day I filled out an application. A week later, I had a job—and a new name.

The employee roster listed names "last name, first name." My last name is long, so only four letters of my first name fit. Ronald became Rona (rhymes with My Sharona). It started as a joke. Then it stuck. Then it became a nickname. And finally—a name that meant something.

"Rona!" they'd call when I walked in, all energy and inside jokes. The sound of it meant laughter, camaraderie, belonging—the things I'd been searching for since moving to the city.

Working at Coconuts didn't feel like work. It was more like hanging out with friends and occasionally helping customers. We were all the same age, perpetually under-caffeinated and over-dramatic, treating that little two-story store like our clubhouse.

When someone paged a call on "Line 3" from the first floor —which didn't exist—it meant someone sketchy was coming up. We'd pretend to alphabetize CDs while watching like secret agents. When the coast was clear, someone would yell, "All clear, Rona!" and we'd laugh until closing time.

After hours, we'd blast whatever CD we were obsessed with that week, vacuum the carpets, restock the shelves, and dance through cleanup like it was an encore. Then we'd spill out into Boystown for food, drinks, and bad decisions.

I don't remember feeling tired after long days at my day job, then rushing to Coconuts. Maybe youth shielded me from exhaustion—or maybe joy did. Even when I arrived grumpy or worn out, someone would yell, "Rona!" and the fatigue would melt away.

That job wasn't just about money or music—it was about finding my people. About discovering that belonging doesn't always announce itself with fanfare. Sometimes it sneaks in through a joke on a name tag.

They called me Rona. And I loved it.

Just like how I loved when Ken called me
"vavy."

Author's Note:

This story always makes me laugh, but what moves me most now isn't the humor—it's what it represents. Rona wasn't just a nickname; it was the first time I felt seen for who I was becoming, not who I was trying to be.

When I moved to Chicago, I was searching for a sense of belonging—a place where my weirdness, my humor, and my heart could all fit in the same room. That little record store gave me that. It was loud, chaotic, and gloriously unfiltered. I didn't have to shrink myself or edit the edges; I could just be me.

Looking back, it's easy to see how much those early experiences shaped me—the joy of connection, the power of community, the importance of showing up as yourself. Even now, when someone calls me Rona—and a few people still do—I can feel that spark of joy all over again. It's a reminder that belonging isn't something you wait for. You build it. One joke, one song, one late-night laugh at a time.

TOYS "R"NT ME

"Ron from BORUS to the break room! Ron from BORUS to the break room!" The deep voice over the Toys "R" Us loudspeaker wasn't a reprimand. It was my bat signal.

I weaved through the stockroom maze, dodging pallets of Power Rangers and Furbys. Holidays at Toys "R" Us in 1993 were full-contact retail. Survival required strategy—and sarcasm.

BORUS (short for Books "R" Us) was a pilot project run by Western Publishing, my actual employer. Technically, I wasn't a Toys "R" Us employee, which meant no uniform, no rulebook, and no expectations. I was a stealth agent in jeans and a smirk, armed with a clipboard I mostly used to look important.

The break room was my refuge—a fluorescent sanctuary where time slowed and no one asked for a price check. It's also where I met Kathy. She ran the cashiers like a general with perfect hair and a killer laugh. Her confidence was magnetic; her humor, disarming. Even in the chaos, she made work feel like a comedy sketch we were all lucky to be in.

I first approached her out of necessity—and a little charm offensive.

"I haven't gotten anyone to sign my vendor sheet in a while," I said, holding out my clipboard. "My boss checks it first thing. Would you mind initialing the last few weeks?"

She raised an eyebrow. "The last few weeks?"

I grinned and fanned out a handful of different colored pens. "So it doesn't look like the same person did them all at once."

Her laugh was instant—loud, joyful, contagious. It bounced off the linoleum walls and sealed our friendship on the spot.

From then on, we were co-conspirators in the trenches: sharing vending machine coffee, gossiping about customers, and finding small ways to rebel against retail monotony. We laughed until our sides hurt, sometimes at the absurdity of it all, sometimes just to survive it.

I didn't know it then, but that was the beginning of one of the longest friendships of my life—one that would outlast a thousand broken toys, two decades of change, and even loss.

Looking back, I see now what I couldn't then: I was searching for belonging long before I could name it. I thought I'd find it through work, through achievement, through the next shiny thing. But what I found—again and again—was people.

Kathy was one of the first who saw me as I was, not who I was trying to be. Together we learned that connection doesn't need grand circumstances. Sometimes it's built in the hum of fluorescent lights and the laughter echoing off a toy aisle at closing time.

We still laugh about those days in the Thunderdome of retail—shrinking violets turned veterans of chaos. Beneath the laughter, there's a quiet truth I've carried ever since:

The universe rarely sends you what you think you need. It sends you who you need. Even if they're wearing a Toys "R" Us name tag.

The logbook that sparked an epic friendship.

Author's Note:

This piece always makes me smile because it captures a time when life was wonderfully unscripted—when I was still figuring out who I was, but finding glimmers of belonging in unexpected places.

Back then, I thought purpose came from achievement—the right job, the right title, the right plan. But standing under fluorescent lights at Toys "R" Us, laughing with Kathy over vending machine coffee, I was learning something far more important: connection is what gives life its shape.

That friendship—born in chaos and held together by laughter—became one of the cornerstones of my adult life. Kathy showed me that humor can be holy, that ordinary days can be sacred, and that the people who meet you where you are can change your story just by showing up.

Even now, decades later, when I think about what I've lost and what I've gained, I come back to this: love, in all its forms—

romantic, platonic, fleeting, lifelong—is what steadies us. Sometimes it finds you in the unlikeliest of places. Sometimes, it finds you between the aisles of a toy store.

BITTERSWEET

Ed was tall. Taller than I was. At six-three, I was used to being the tallest guy in the room—or at least in the gay bars of my college town or the few clubs I'd been to in Indianapolis. But this was Chicago. The big time.

Ed had to be six-five, with dark hair, a disarming smile, and the kind of easy charisma that made people lean in. I noticed him immediately—the way he laughed, the way he owned the space without trying. When I edged near enough, his attention shifted from his friend to me, and the air between us changed.

It was the summer of 1993, and I was twenty-five—young, restless, and reckless in all the ways you can only be once. I'd driven from Indiana on a whim, wearing my favorite outfit: green tie with white polka dots, white button-down, cuffed jean shorts, and ankle boots with scrunched socks. A look. I was living at my aunt and uncle's house, driving three hours each way to my assistant manager job at Blockbuster, and spending what little I had chasing connection—or maybe escape.

That night, the bar was alive—humid, loud, full of possibility. I asked Ed to dance. Maybe it was courage, maybe it was loneliness, but when he said yes, I felt something loosen in me. After a few songs, he leaned close and said, "How about another cocktail?"

The chemistry was easy. We moved from bar to bar, talking and laughing, brushing hands, trading glances that said more than we were ready to. When we finally stepped outside, the streets were strangely quiet—Market Days had ended, and the city felt like it belonged to us.

At the last bar, after one too many syrupy shots, Ed said, "Let's go home."

"Where do you live?" I asked.

"Bittersweet," he said.

Bittersweet. It sounded like foreshadowing, but youth and vodka made me brave.

His apartment was full of warmth—roommates laughing, half-eaten pizza, the hum of a TV. Ordinary, safe. He disappeared into the bathroom and came back to bed, and soon we were kissing, tangled together in a way that felt like both discovery and relief. When I realized he didn't have a condom, I froze.

"It's okay," he said.

But it wasn't. Not in 1993. Not in the age of AIDS.

He sniffed something from a little brown bottle and offered it to me. "I don't do drugs," I said.

He smiled softly. "Then I'll be a gentleman." And he was. We fell asleep spooned together, his breath steady against the back of my neck.

In the morning, he invited me to join him and his roommates for some sightseeing. I told him I couldn't—I had to get back to Indiana, back to my impossible life. He kissed me goodbye at the door. I remember the quiet sweetness of it, the way sunlight hit his hair.

A year later, I'd finally made the move to Chicago. One chilly fall morning, I stopped into Roscoe's for soup and picked up Gay Chicago Magazine. Flipping through the pages, I saw his photo. Smiling, handsome, familiar.

Ed.

The obituary said he'd died from "complications related to AIDS." The phrase I'd read so many times it barely registered—until it did. Until it was him.

The shock was physical. My stomach dropped. The world blurred. I remembered the laughter, the way he looked at me, the way I'd said no. How close I'd come to saying yes.

Over the years, I've thought about him often. Not with fear, but gratitude. For his kindness. For his gentleness. For the lesson I didn't know I was learning that night—to trust my instincts, to listen to the small, steady voice that tells you when something isn't right.

I can't picture his face clearly anymore, but I can still feel his presence—that warmth, that easy laughter. There's an old saying: if someone remembers you, you never truly die.

So when I think of Ed, I like to believe he's still there—on that street called Bittersweet—reminding me how fragile and precious it all was.

When I told Ken this story, he was incredibly
sweet about it. We had a quiet moment in
honor of Ed.

Author's Note:

Writing *Bittersweet* brought me face-to-face with the version of myself who was still learning to listen to his own voice—the one who wanted to belong so badly he often ignored instinct in favor of possibility.

That night with Ed changed me in ways I couldn't have articulated back then. It taught me that courage doesn't always look like saying yes. Sometimes it's found in restraint—in trusting your intuition when everything around you tells you to surrender it.

But more than that, it reminded me how fragile and beautiful connection can be. Ed wasn't a chapter I expected to revisit, but when I did, I realized the story wasn't about fear or survival. It was about compassion—for him, and for the younger me who was still fumbling his way toward self-understanding in a world that didn't make it easy.

Remembering Ed—his laughter, his warmth, his humanity—

felt like honoring all the lives touched by that era's quiet devastation. And, in a way, it honored the version of me who walked away from that night both lucky and changed.

The sweetness, the sadness—they coexist. That's what makes it bittersweet.

PART V: THE RETURN OF JOY

LEARNING THE ART OF LIVING FOR THE FUTURE WHILE HONORING THE PAST

NECESSITY IS THE
MOTHER OF REINVENTION

Life is funny. Not ha-ha funny. Just...strange. I never expected to fall in love for the first time at thirty-one, or to be a widower two weeks before my forty-third birthday. I never expected that the same loss that broke me would also lead me to the most fulfilling chapter of my life.

It's the paradox of grief: the very pain that shattered my world also revealed my power, my purpose, and my passion. Out of loss came discovery. Out of devastation came reinvention.

Losing him wasn't my choice. But everything after that was.

Sometimes I wonder who I'd be if I hadn't gone through it. As much as I resisted the label 'widower,' grief became my greatest teacher. Those early blog posts and late-night journal entries—my lifeline—were where I met the version of myself I'd been avoiding. Each sentence was a step forward, even when I didn't know where forward was.

Grief gave me traits I didn't know I had: resilience, empathy, humor, and a refusal to hide what I feel. It taught me to keep my heart open even when it hurt.

Ken's death wasn't unexpected. By the time we met in 2001, he'd already survived cancer three times. When it returned in 2009, we still believed he'd beat it again. He even chose a radical hemipelvectomy—removing the rest of his leg and part of his pelvis—to buy time. That was Ken. Courageous. Hopeful. Utterly unwilling to surrender to anything but life.

And for a while, it worked. Until it didn't.

When he took his final breaths in our living room after nine weeks of home hospice, I whispered, "Go on to your next adventure." Every great adventure had been with him. Now, there was no guide. Just me—broken, lost, but still breathing.

You don't get over losing someone you love. You build around the hole they leave. It's both impossible and inevitable. You learn to live beside the ache. You carry their love forward as you make something new from what's left. For a while, I wore 'widower' like armor—a badge that proved he'd been here. But over time, it began to feel heavy. I packed up his things into a box labeled Relics and set it aside. I clung to old routines as if repetition might conjure him back.

It wasn't until I moved out of the apartment where he'd died and into a place of my own that I felt something shift. For the first time, I wasn't following anyone's lead. I was writing a new story—one with a single author.

After nearly a decade in the same job, surrounded by kind people but stagnant work, I knew it was time. Writing had always been my compass—ever since I was thirteen and first discovered the quiet magic of words. When an opportunity came to move into a communications role, I jumped.

After Ken died, there was an impatience inside me I couldn't ignore anymore—a voice growing louder by the day. Maybe it was one of Ken's parting gifts. It pushed me to move, to change, to write. With some hard-won networking, I found a new role where I get to do just that. I write every day now. I've built a reputation as a communicator, a storyteller—a wordsmith with purpose. A 'word ninja,' as I once called myself in my blog.

It felt like coming home. Writing in my own voice, not corporate jargon. Creating, connecting, communicating. It was terrifying—and freeing. Writing has always been my safest risk. It tells me the truth, even when I don't want to hear it. That's what this essay is, really: a love letter to reinvention. To the courage that comes from loss. To building a life that feels fully mine.

Sometimes guilt still sneaks in—when I realize how happy I am, how full my life has become. I'm not grateful for losing Ken. But I am grateful for what grief revealed: the capacity to start again. To create. To thrive.

Ken was my fiercest champion. He still is. I see his influence in every brave step I take, every risk I write into existence. His legacy lives in my courage, my compassion, and my pen.

It's easy to be bolder when you feel loved and supported.

Author's Note:

This piece marks a turning point—the moment my story shifts from surviving to living. Writing it felt like exhaling after holding my breath for years.

For so long, I thought of grief as something I had to endure, something to outlast. What I eventually learned was that it's also a creative force—destructive, yes, but also deeply generative. It clears the ground for what's next.

Ken's death didn't just change my life; it changed my capacity to shape it. It stripped away everything that wasn't essential until all that remained was purpose—the quiet knowing that words were my way through. Writing gave me a framework to rebuild, one sentence at a time.

I used to think reinvention meant becoming someone new. But now I see it differently. It's about becoming more yourself— the version that's been waiting under all the noise and fear.

This essay isn't about loss, really. It's about what loss revealed. The part of me that's brave enough to begin again.

THE OLD CAMPING
PERCOLATOR RIDES AGAIN

While cleaning out my apartment to prepare to move into my first condo, I found our old camping percolator and enamel-speckled coffee cups. The sight stopped me cold. It wasn't just a coffee pot—it was a time machine. One look, and I was back in Ojai: smoky air, morning chill, Ken beside me, his laughter echoing through the canyon.

The wave hit fast—reminding me there would be no more sunrise coffee, no more burnt marshmallows, no more middle-of-the-night tent collapses. I packed the gear away and shut the closet door. Out of sight, maybe—but not out of heart.

The percolator had been a gift from my friend Kathy after she joined us on that now-legendary Ojai weekend camping trip in 2005. Watching us pour boiling water from a tin pan through a flimsy paper filter balanced on a glass pitcher, she declared it "a tragedy waiting to happen." She wasn't wrong. The percolator—sturdy, simple, vintage—became a fixture on every trip after that.

I stood in front of the camping gear for a long time, my hand hovering over the donation pile. The tent. The stove. The things that only made sense because of him. I tried to picture myself using them alone and came up empty. Camping without Ken felt like erasing the point of it altogether. I almost gave it all away. Almost. But at the last minute, something in me refused to let go. Not because I was ready to use it again. Not because I had a plan. Just because I wasn't ready to say that final goodbye. Not yet.

Then, life—still capable of surprise—handed me something unexpected: a new friend who enjoys camping. When we discovered that shared love, we planned a weekend trip. I hesitated at first, unsure what ghosts might join us. But curiosity won out.

Packing the car, I unearthed that same percolator—its handle worn smooth from years of fireside mornings—some with Ken and me, and many more from unknown previous owners. I half expected the grief to ambush me, but instead I felt proud. Ken had labeled every container, stocked foil and salt—even tucked in toilet paper. Even now, he was taking care of me.

Setting up the tent took twice as long as I remembered—and twice the patience. Once inside, it felt familiar. Cozy. Safe. Only now there was Netflix streaming from an iPad—a modern luxury that would've made Ken laugh.

I'd wondered if the trip would hurt. It did, in small ways— grief still likes to tap me on the shoulder—but it didn't undo me. The memories didn't drown me; they steadied me.

The weekend was simple: biking, campfires, laughter, quiet. And in that quiet, I felt something shift. Time hadn't erased the grief; it had simply softened its edges, leaving behind something gentler. Gratitude, maybe. Or grace. Ken was still there—in the way the gear was packed, in the little efficiencies he'd built into our routine, in the words I caught myself saying out loud that were really his.

That trip wasn't about reliving the past. It was about reclaiming a joy I thought I'd lost. The percolator hissed and burbled on the camp stove just like it always had. And for the first time in a long time, the sound didn't break me.

It filled me.

This trip wasn't an ending. It was another beginning.

It doesn't get as much use these days as it used too, but it's still in my camping supplies.

Author's Note:

This essay is about what healing actually looks like—quiet, ordinary, and often disguised as something else. A weekend away. A cup of coffee. A decision to try again.

For a long time, I thought grief would always be a wall between my past and my future. What I've learned instead is that it becomes a bridge—connecting who I was with who I'm still becoming. The camping trip wasn't about replacing Ken or rewriting the story we shared; it was about stepping back into a part of life I'd sealed off, trusting that I could hold both the ache and the joy.

The percolator, once a relic, became a reminder that love doesn't end—it changes form. It shows up in how we carry the memories forward, how we honor the person we lost by continuing to live fully.

Every time I use it now, I think less about what's gone and more about what remains: the laughter, the lessons, the small rituals that still feel like home. That's what reinvention really is —not a rejection of the past, but a reunion with the parts of it that are still alive in you.

THE PUPPY WHO SAVED ME

Getting a puppy is a big step. For anyone. Getting Kallie was an even bigger one for me, because bringing her into my life was the first real step I took toward moving forward after Ken died.

They say not to make any big decisions for at least a year after losing someone you love. Ken died on June 1, 2011. Kallie arrived in my life on June 18, 2012. At the time, I was on a leave of absence from work. I'd gone back too soon after Ken died and never really stopped long enough to catch my breath. I moved through those early months on autopilot, doing what was expected, functioning just enough to pass. Grief waited patiently for me to slow down. When I finally did, I had no idea what was supposed to come next.

In January of 2012, I started thinking about getting a dog. Not just any dog. I was only interested in a female Chow Chow. That decision had been made years earlier by Quantum, Ken's beautiful girl, who had learned to love me as the three of us became a family during our ten years together. Back then, I needed throughlines—bridges from my life with Ken to my life without him. I wasn't ready to let go of everything we had built.

That spring, I searched and searched. Nothing. Dead ends. Listings that disappeared. Breeders who never responded. It felt like another closed door, and I stopped trying. Then, the weekend of my birthday in June, I was visiting my parents. Before going to bed Saturday night, I did one more search. And this time, out of nowhere, there she was—a breeder in northern Illinois, appearing like Brigadoon after months of nothing. I emailed her, expecting silence. Instead, she replied that she had one girl left. Just one. She attached a photo.

I drove home on Sunday. On Monday, after a trip to PetSmart that felt both practical and ceremonial, I got in the car and went to meet her. When the breeder's daughter placed a squirming black fluff ball in my arms, she stopped moving almost immediately and fell fast asleep. As if she knew. As if she'd arrived where she was meant to be.

I met her parents. A few of her siblings. Then I tucked her into the crate in the back seat and started the drive home. The deep, ferocious bark she'd grow into later was, at that point, just an occasional squeak from the back seat.

Having a puppy is a full-time job. Kallie tore through that apartment—and my ankles—like a black, saw-toothed blur. House-training was easy. Crate-training was a disaster. Eventually, I gave up and let her sleep in bed with me. On those warm summer nights, as she snored beside me, I'd whisper into the dark, "You saved me, Kallie."

And she did.

She saved me by giving me something to focus on besides my own grief. By needing me. By pulling me back into the role of caregiver when I wasn't sure who I was anymore. I'd taken care of Ken with everything I had. Loving Kallie gave that instinct somewhere to land instead of turning inward and consuming me.

She distracted me with boundless energy, with kisses and

chaos and joy, until I slowly emerged from the year-long, self-imposed social hibernation I hadn't even realized I was in. Unlike Quantum, with her breed-appropriate indifference to strangers, Kallie was a social butterfly. The dog park. Daycare. Neighborhood walks. She loved it all. She dragged me—sometimes literally—out of my own isolation and into conversations with neighbors, friendships with other dogs and their people. She reintroduced me to the world.

She moved with me from the apartment Ken and I had shared into a loft condo two blocks away. She welcomed new friends as I built a small neighborhood tribe. She was my steady co-pilot when I moved in with my boyfriend at the time while house-hunting, and then into our little Mid-Century Modern in the suburbs, where she finally got the yard I'd been promising her since she was a squeaking pup in a crate.

Kallie was my conscience. My daemon, for anyone familiar with Phillip Pullman's *His Dark Materials*, is the physical embodiment of my soul walking beside me. Quantum had been that for Ken. Kallie was that for me.

But more than symbolism or metaphor, she was my best friend. My constant. My companion as we settled into a life that wasn't dramatic or flashy, but deeply, quietly shared. Loving her was easy. Losing her was not.

Still, it's worth every second of pain that comes with loving someone deeply. The pain doesn't compare to the hours and days and months—and, if we're lucky, years—of joy that come before it. Connection is the most essential part of being human. It's why we risk our hearts in the first place.

When I knew it was time to free her from her failing body, I lay on the floor of the vet's office with her, holding her close, whispering through my tears, "You saved me, Kallie. You saved me."

Because she did.

Thank you, Kalpurnia 'Kallie' Kismet Derson Stempkowski. I will love you and be grateful for you forever.

That was my first glimpse of Kallie.

Author's Note:

When I first wrote this piece, I thought it was about Kallie. And in a way, it still is. But now, I see it's also about what comes after survival—how love, in its gentlest form, coaxes us back into living.

Kallie didn't replace Ken. She reminded me how to exist in a world without him. She gave shape to my days when everything else felt shapeless. Through her, I learned that healing isn't a single moment of transformation—it's a series of small acts of care that eventually add up to hope.

Every walk, every shared meal, every quiet night on the couch rebuilt something in me that grief had broken. She turned devotion into motion, love into forward momentum.

Grief taught me endurance. Kallie taught me joy. And

maybe that's what love does at its best—it keeps teaching us, even after the lesson should be over.

A NIGHT TO REMEMBER

Since saying goodbye to my sweet Kallie, I've been thinking a lot about her, Ken, and Quantum—the three souls most tied to my heart. They never met, but they're deeply connected. Quantum was the beginning of it all, the dog who turned me into a devoted Chow Chow dad. Kallie came later, my constant companion through the quiet years. And Ken—he was the love that made all the rest make sense. I used to tell Kallie stories about her 'big sister', Quantum, and her 'papa Kenny.' She'd tilt her head, as if she understood every word.

Losing Kallie reawakened the grief I thought had softened. Losing her was losing a little more of Ken, too—though he would've hated that phrasing. "Don't say you lost me," he'd say. "Parents lose a child in a grocery store. Just say I died." His humor never wavered, even at the end. And he wasn't wrong. He may have died, but he was never lost. Not to me.

The other night, scrolling through old photos, I stumbled on one I hadn't seen in years: Ken, relaxed and smiling, playing Trivial Pursuit in the guesthouse where we lived at the time, Quantum asleep beside him. Just seeing it hit me like music you didn't know you missed until the first note plays.

That little guesthouse in Los Angeles—our first home together—was full of sunlight and laughter and simple joys like this one. I love that photo not just for Ken's handsome face, but for the tenderness in how he looked at Quantum. It captures the gentleness that defined him.

Old photos have a way of showing up right when you need them. They remind you that the moments that seem ordinary are the ones that end up meaning everything.

People sometimes wonder if I live in the past. Maybe I do—but I don't apologize for it. That part of my life was extraordinary, and its echoes are part of who I am. Looking back isn't about being stuck there; it's about understanding how those moments shaped the life I have now.

Meeting Ken awakened something in me that I didn't fully understand while he was alive—but losing him brought it into focus. His death revealed parts of me I hadn't known were there: resilience, openness, and a kind of courage that only love —and loss—can teach.

Writing has always been how I hold on. It keeps what I love from drifting too far into memory. It turns moments into something permanent—something that breathes. That night in the photo—just a game, a laugh, a sleeping dog—wasn't extraordinary at all. But it was everything.

And maybe that's the point: some nights don't fade. They live on, quietly, outside of time.

This moment from that night still feels so close.

Author's Note:

This essay began as a photo—one image that opened a door. What I found on the other side wasn't just nostalgia; it was presence. Writing about Ken, Quantum, and Kallie reminded me that memory isn't a static place we visit—it's a living space we carry within us.

For years, I believed healing meant letting go. What I've come to understand is that it's more about holding differently. The people—and pets—we've loved don't leave our story; their chapter just changes form. They keep teaching us, long after the plot has moved on.

In this piece, the ordinary becomes sacred: a game, a laugh, a dog asleep at someone's feet. I think that's the quiet miracle of grief—it sharpens our awareness of small moments, showing us how much life is contained in what seems unremarkable.

Writing helps me keep those moments alive, not as relics, but as reminders of what endures: love, humor, and the simple truth that the past isn't gone. It's still here—woven into the present, whispering, remember this.

THE POWER OF YES

Over the years, I've said yes to a lot of things I never expected to. The most memorable ones began in my life with Ken. He was so daring. As a cancer survivor who had faced his own mortality, there was no time like the present for Ken. "Right now is all we're guaranteed," he'd purr in that deep voice of his. Some broke me open. Some helped me heal. But every yes carried me a little closer to the life I have now—a life still stitched with Ken's love, but also wide open to whatever's next.

During the summer of 2025, I began thinking about what would have been Ken's milestone 60th birthday in September. And something inside me 'clicked.' It was almost audible. I needed to acknowledge—to celebrate—his life and legacy with a fundraiser that would help people impacted by cancer. It was something that was *so him*, and, in fact, *so me*.

While putting together all the details of this fundraiser, I'd been thinking a lot about the power of saying yes. It's such a simple word—three letters, one syllable—but it can crack open whole new worlds—especially when you say it even though you're terrified. Or maybe because you're terrified.

That's how I felt when Ken asked me to run lights and

sound for his one-man show, My Foot Left. Let's be clear: I had zero experience doing anything like that. My tech résumé at the time consisted of knowing where the light switches were and being able to press play on a boombox without breaking a sweat.

So, of course, I said yes.

Because of Ken's sparkle, he made "yes" feel less like a risk and more like an adventure (as I would later learn, everything with Ken was an adventure of the best kind). He didn't push; he inspired. He believed in people so fiercely that it made you start to believe in yourself—or at the very least, made you want to rise to the occasion so you didn't let him down.

And here's the thing: saying yes didn't magically make me good at lights and sound. There may have been a few rogue lighting cues and questionable volume levels—sorry, Ken—but it made me part of something magical. It gave me a front-row seat (well, more like a back-of-the-theater folding chair) to the story of someone I loved and admired deeply, and the chance to help bring it to life. That yes turned into one of the most meaningful experiences of my life.

Ken always said, "Enjoy the journey." Not in that saccharine, stitched-on-a-pillow kind of way—but as a real invitation to be present, to be open, to be willing. Even when it's hard. Even when you feel wildly underqualified. Even when you're scared.

Especially when you're scared.

So, here's my reminder—to you, and to myself: say yes. Say it even when your voice shakes. Say it even when you don't know what comes next. Because the best parts of life—the meaningful parts, the joyful parts, the stories you'll tell decades later—are often hiding just on the other side of yes.

Say yes to joining us for the digital premiere of My Foot Left. Say yes to honoring Ken's story, his humor, his resilience, and his giant heart. And if you're able, say yes to donating in his memory—because your gift helps keep his light shining and supports those still navigating their own cancer journeys.

⚡ Lights up.
🦋 Sound on.
🕊 Let's go.

The wrap party for Ken's show. I was never prouder to have said yes!

Author's Note:

When I started writing these essays, I didn't know where they'd lead. I only knew I needed to find words big enough to hold everything I'd lived through—love, loss, laughter, and the long, uneven road that follows both grief and grace.

Each story became a small act of remembering and rebuilding. A way of keeping Ken close while also learning how to carry him differently. Along the way, I rediscovered not just the weight of loss, but the light that comes after—the kind that shows up quietly at first, then grows every time you choose to say yes to life again.

Something about this essay and planning to honor what would have been Ken's 60th birthday freed something inside me. I loved all the planning, marketing, fundraising and preparation for this YouTube Premiere—something I'd never done before. I'm not saying goodbye to him, but I'm saying goodbye to the version of me who struggled desperately for years to remain connected with him. The connection remains, but there is so much more I want to do and other people I want to connect with.

If you've made it to this page, thank you—for reading, for feeling, for bearing witness. I hope somewhere in these pages you found something that helped you feel a little less alone.

Because in the end, that's what stories do. They remind us that even when everything changes, love doesn't disappear—it just keeps finding new ways to show up.

EPILOGUE

If there's one thing grief has taught me, it's that endings rarely arrive cleanly. They blur and echo. They fold back on themselves until you realize that what you thought was an ending was really an invitation—to begin again, differently.

When I first started writing these essays, I thought I was documenting loss. I see now that I've been documenting life—its texture, its ache, its humor, its absurd beauty. Grief was merely the doorway I walked through to find it.

Each story here began as a way to remember: Ken, my family, the people and moments that built me. But memory, like love, doesn't stay put. It shapeshifts. It keeps us company. It keeps us honest. It reminds us that even when everything we know is gone, we still have a voice—and that voice can create light.

For a long time, I was afraid to stop writing about Ken. I thought if I did, I'd lose him again. But now I understand that writing about the rest of my life doesn't erase him—it extends him. His influence hums underneath everything I do. It's in the journals I fill, the gardens I plant, the friends I make, the dog I loved.

We don't move on from the people we love. We move with them—carrying their laughter, their lessons, their fingerprints on our hearts. We become the proof that they mattered.

That's the luck we carry. Not luck that spares us pain, but luck that insists on grace inside it. Luck that shows up in the middle of ordinary days—in the quiet kindness of a stranger, the warmth of a memory, or the sound of your own laughter returning after a long silence.

When I look back now, I don't see a life defined by loss. I see a life shaped by it, yes—but also expanded, softened, deepened. I see a man who learned to keep showing up.

And maybe that's the truest measure of survival:
To keep showing up.
To keep writing.
To keep loving.

Because no matter how heavy it feels, love is always what remains.

Early in our relationship, on the beach in
Malibu.

ABOUT THE AUTHOR

Ron Stempkowski is an award-winning writer whose work explores grief, love, and the strange, beautiful ways we find our way forward. After losing his husband, Ken, to cancer, Ron began writing as a way to make sense of a world that no longer made sense. What started as survival slowly became a calling—to tell stories that help others feel less alone. His essays have been praised for their humor, heart, and unflinching honesty.

He's also the creator of *Twisted Plot Paper*, a journaling brand that helps people use writing as a tool for healing and self-discovery.

Ron lives in Park Ridge, Illinois, where he serves on the board of the Friends of the Park Ridge Public Library and can often be found writing in a local coffee shop: journal open, fountain pen in hand, chasing the next sentence that feels true.

Learn more at **ronstempkowski.com**.

instagram.com/ronstempkowski
linkedin.com/in/ronstempkowski
youtube.com/ronstempkowski